ON THE BORDER *of* SNOW AND MELT

ON THE BORDER *of* SNOW AND MELT

Selected Poems of Georgy Ivanov

Introduction by Stanislav Shvabrin

Translated, Edited, and Annotated
by Jerome Katsell and Stanislav Shvabrin

PERCEVAL PRESS

On the Border of Snow and Melt
ISBN 978-0-9774869-4-6
©2011 Perceval Press

Perceval Press
1223 Wilshire Blvd., Suite F
Santa Monica, CA 90403
www.percevalpress.com

Introduction © 2011 Stanislav Shvabrin
Translation, Editorship, Annotation © 2011 by Jerome Katsell
and Stanislav Shvabrin
English Copy Editor: Sherri Schottlaender

Design: Michele Perez
Cover photo: Lenka Minkowski, 2010
Page 14: Yury Annenkov, *Portrait of Georgy Ivanov* (1921)

CONTENTS

from ОТПЛЫТИЕ НА ОСТРОВ ЦИТЕРУ /
from EMBARKATION FOR THE ISLAND OF CYTHERA (1937)

ПОРТРЕТ БЕЗ СХОДСТВА / A PORTRAIT WITHOUT LIKENESS (1950)

СТИХИ / POEMS (1943–1958)

ПОСМЕРТНЫЙ ДНЕВНИК / POSTHUMOUS DIARY (1958)

BEYOND THE BORDER *of* SNOW AND MELT:
THE AFTERLIFE OF GEORGY IVANOV'S LYRICISM

As Georgy Ivanov, that quintessential antihero of Russian poetry, is getting ready to introduce himself to his English-language readers, serious doubts may—and should—be raised as to whether he is worthy of a handshake in the first place.[1] There is no question that, when presented quite impartially, a number of facts about his biography will attest to his propensity toward behaving in the manner of an outright scoundrel. It is his poetry, however—or a peculiar brand of lyricism characteristic of his poetry, to be precise—that against all odds (and certainly in stark contrast to Ivanov's seemingly irrepressible urge to disgust his readers and dismay his scholars) carries him through, making the sparse poetic output of this deeply divisive figure a phenomenon, a territory that deserves not only to be discovered, but also revisited. A novice Ivanov reader soon enough realizes that a meaningful conversation with this man of letters renders excessive formality unnecessary, or rather simply irrelevant, but then if one is to be appreciative of the recent advances in matters aesthetic, one ought to be grateful for knowing better than to treat literature—least of all poetry—as an area where only small talk is permitted, a venue where one is sure not to be insulted out of one's comfortable agnosticism in such areas of human enterprise as love and hate, life, and death (not to mention the courage and cowardice with which one acts when faced with the task of defining one's position on these not-so-abstract notions). Still, even in this time and age there is something of a miracle about the afterlife that Ivanov's lyricism (but certainly not his biography and deeds) has been enjoying ever since his death in 1958. Ivanov, the poet who with astonishing audacity, indeed defiance, spoke of his imminent, though distant, redemption and resurrection—and who did so while finding himself in the lower depths of despair with precious little chance of salvaging his life work from total oblivion—*that* Ivanov, curiously enough, has been proven right about the way in which he assured everyone (but first and foremost himself, one senses) on his deathbed: "I haven't forgotten, that to me it is promised / To rise again. To return to Russia—in my poems" (see the poem that opens with the line "The nightingale's trill in the oleander branches" in this volume). While Ivanov's return to Russia has not been triumphant, no one would argue against its being irreversible in the same way as no one should claim that there was any need for fanfare.

---

1 For an early selection of some of Ivanov's best poems in English versions by Theodore Weiss and Ron Loewinsohn, see "Double Vision: Two American Poets Translate Georgy Ivanov," in *The Bitter Air of Exile: Russian Writers in the West, 1922–1972*, ed. Simon Karlinsky and Alfred Appel Jr. (Berkeley: University of California Press, 1973), 164–68.

The Russia to which Ivanov has returned and the Russia into which his lyricism has been resurrected is a concept more metaphysical than geographic or spatial; Ivanov's lyricism has found him a reader, who, much like the best of Ivanov's poetry, is in no need of a geographic or political affiliation, being, just like Ivanov's lyricism, extra-territorial. All the more reason to go beyond Ivanov's dependence on Russian as the sole means of embodying his lyricism and to endeavor to overcome the linguistic boundary that confines his verse exclusively to the Russian language.

Consider the poem reproduced below. On its surface it has two plotlines, one running parallel to the other, yet neither finding a decisive resolution at the poem's end. The first one can be said to be more contemplative and descriptive; it captures something of a stream of consciousness, a train of associative thoughts. If the reader were to ignore the constantly intruding parenthetic insertions dotting the poem's text, the momentum of the poem's first line would carry the reader past a few flash-backs from the protagonist's present that then quickly lead up to those from his past. It is easy, however, to ignore the poem's second plotline, one pointing toward some sort of a future resolution or dénouement:

A bluish cloud
(A chill at my temple)
A bluish cloud
And still more clouds . . .

And an ancient apple tree
(Perhaps I should wait awhile?)
The simple-hearted apple tree
Bursting into bloom again.

It all looks so Russian—
(Smile and pull it!)
This narrow cloud
Just like a small boat with children.

And so astonishingly blue
(With the first strike of the clock . . .)
That hopeless line
Of endless forests.

What may not be apparent in the first reading of this poem surely does come into sharper focus when it is reread. If the two plotlines competing for the reader's attention were to intersect, that would be at a point where the narrator will pull the trigger of a gun, the cool muzzle of which is pressed to his temple in the poem's first stanza. This poem is about a suicide attempt contemplated, but not quite carried out, by the protagonist, and the topic (as well as its thematic entourage) is a central motif in Ivanov's poetry. The protagonist of Ivanov's mature poems—his demeanor and preferred set of references quickly betray him as a Russian émigré living in pre- and post–World War II Europe with no hope of returning to his homeland in his lifetime and with no desire to be integrated into his adopted community—constantly toys with the idea. The poet himself, however, especially at the later stages in the development of his lyricism, makes no secret of the fear that grips him when it is time to make a transition from a declaration to a practical step:

> I'm not against "crossing over" either,
> But still I'm afraid. I admit it.
> (see "The longer I live, the less," p. 373)

Ivanov's mature lyricism pivoted on a peak where triumph and shame converge at their most exalted and unexpected moments, where boldness and cowardice suddenly intersect—little wonder, then, that an early observer claimed that he was an existentialist *par excellence*, an existentialist sans a Saint-Germain abode and global fame.[2]

Much like the suicidal protagonist of the poem above, Georgy Ivanov chose to spend his entire life living on the border of choices he did not have the courage to make, successfully turning this no-man's-land into a metaphysical domain of his own. A late arrival at the flourishing of pre-Revolutionary Russian culture that is known today as its Silver Age, Ivanov spent a considerable amount of time as an apprentice to Innokenty Annensky, Aleksandr Blok, Mikhail Kuzmin, and Nikolay Gumilyov, to name but a few significant names. He honed the poetic technique that burst into late bloom only when the Russia of his childhood and youth had ceased to exist.

Georgy Ivanov—Geórgii Vladímirovich Ivánov (in Russian, Гео́ргий Влади́мирович Ива́нов; as a sign of the poet's aristocratic origin, his last name is stressed on the second, not last, syllable, as would be the case with incalculable bearers of the otherwise identical last name, the Russian equivalent of "Johnson")—was born on October 29, 1894, in present-day Lithuania. Ivanov spent his formative years in St. Petersburg, becoming and remaining for the rest of his days a denizen of Petersburg to the marrow of his bones (a living anachronism, that is, for most of his life).

Even though Ivanov spent his entire life carefully crafting a perception of himself as a scion of an ancient aristocratic clan (his widow Irina Odoevtseva also makes considerable effort to support this myth in her popular memoirs), the future poet's

2 See Roman Gul', "Georgii Ivanov" [introduction], in Georgii Ivanov, *1943–1958. Stikhi* (New York: Izdanie "Novogo zhurnala," 1958) 6.

family background was that of a fairly unremarkable member of the provincial gentry. Due to his family's financial constraints, Ivanov was allowed to study at a military school with his educational expenses covered by the state out of respect for his father's military service. In St. Petersburg the young cadet quickly fell behind in his studies and eventually abandoned his military education. He had become enthralled with poetry after getting caught in the whirlwind of artistic enterprise that was in the air of the city's last decades as the capital of a seemingly impregnable empire. Ivanov attempted to write poetry himself and listed among his personal acquaintances such accomplished and recognized poets as Blok, Kuzmin, and Sergei Gorodetsky, easily—too easily, perhaps—gaining entry into the world of Russian letters.

Ivanov's debut verse collection, *Embarkation for the Isle of Cythera*, was published late in 1911. On the strength of his promise Ivanov was invited to join the Guild of Poets headed by Gorodetsky and Nikolai Gumilyov, which Ivanov did, breaking with the circle of Ego-Futurists revolving around its minor sun, the madly popular (though not particularly respected among the poetic cognoscenti) Igor Severianin. An unlikely participant in poetic movements or member of literary associations, Ivanov dutifully took part in the activities of the Guild, becoming friends with Gumilyov and coming into contact with a close circle of Gumilyov's associates, among whom were such defining voices of soon-to-come twentieth-century Russian literature as Anna Akhmatova and Osip Mandelstam, whose influence on Ivanov is undeniable. As a Guild member, Ivanov met Georgy Adamovich, who was to become his close literary associate and friend, as well as occasional foe.

Having secured the validation of his older colleagues and new friends who replaced for him his dysfunctional family, Ivanov partook of the flamboyant cabaret culture of the day, becoming a fixture at the Stray Dog, St. Petersburg's leading artistic nightclub. In 1914 he published his second collection oriented towards not only the poetics expected of the members of the Guild of Poets, but also of Acmeism, a fugitive literary movement and brainchild of Gorodetsky and Gumilyov that included Akhmatova and Mandelstam, among others. On the strength of his ties with the Acmeists, Ivanov was admitted into the circle around *Apollo*, a prestigious magazine that became a major bastion of Acmeism, a literary school in the making and desperately seeking to differentiate itself from Symbolism, of which it was an offshoot. Attempting to reject the Symbolist preoccupation with ineffable transcendental verities and the language suitable for their contemplation, Acmeism was conceived by its instigators as the poetry of the phenomenal world, a novel vehicle of expression permeated not by a tragic rift with reality, but a joyous acceptance of it. Having absorbed the tenets of this exciting new doctrine, Ivanov became adept at following in the wake of his mentors. His taste was praised by allies and critics alike, his technique was weighed and found to be impeccable, yet at that stage no one thought of accusing him of originality.

A foretaste of Ivanov's signature lack of concern for what other people might think and say about him came in 1915, when upon securing a deferral from active duty, he released a collection of militaristic poems tellingly entitled *A Monument of Glory*. Even back in those days Ivanov knew perfectly well whose last refuge patriotism is, but the publisher of a series of lowbrow, chauvinistic magazines paid well, and the poet (following the example of his older friend and model Mikhail Kuzmin) was not above accepting the going rate.

After the Bolshevik coup of 1917, during the years of economic devastation, wars, and gradual stifling of civil liberties by the new power, Ivanov participated in the literary life of St. Petersburg-Petrograd, a city stripped of its lofty status and glamour but still immensely rich in cultural potential. Any shadow of illusion about the possibility of finding a satisfactory mode of cohabitation with the Bolsheviks was dispelled in 1921, the year Aleksandr Blok died of neglect for his health and Gumilyov was arrested and shot as part of a Bolshevik reprisal campaign for a failed uprising of sailors in the naval fortress city of Kronstadt. In 1922 Ivanov secured permission to leave Soviet Russia, soon to be followed by his second wife, Irina Odoevtseva, herself a promising poet of the Gumilyov circle.

In 1923 the couple settled in Paris, where Ivanov became one of the most visible and controversial figures in the buoyant cultural life of the Russian anti-Bolshevik diaspora. It was in Paris that a circle of aspiring émigré writers and poets began to form around Ivanov and his old friend Adamovich, both of whom were quick to assume the position of arbiters. Capitalizing on their living links with the key representatives of Russia's pre-Revolutionary culture, Ivanov and Adamovich cleverly used the nostalgia that possessed their younger colleagues as a way to accumulate power, which they used to create—and destroy—reputations. From the nineteen-twenties onward, Ivanov entered into a number of feuds and launched campaigns against offending parties to settle petty scores. Rushing to Adamovich's aid, Ivanov assailed the poet, writer, critic, and scholar Vladislav Khodasevich, quite wrongly citing his lack of genuine talent. Notoriously, Ivanov went on a scurrilous offensive against Vladimir Nabokov (who then published under the pseudonym "Sirin"), dismissing the most talented and original writer to emerge from the Russian diaspora as an epigone of some (unnamed) Western models. (Having once written a disparaging review of Odoevtseva's prose and having withstood an outburst of Ivanov's spiteful rage, Nabokov dispassionately maintained that Ivanov was an "outstanding" [*nezauriadnyi*] poet). Ivanov's alliance with Adamovich, however, turned out to be ill-fated, as their friendship did not stand the test of time.[3]

---

3 In addition to targeting Ivanov in his epigrams, Nabokov composed a lively—and damning—fictional parody of Adamovich's and Ivanov's shady and shameless magazine financing practices. Nabokov's short story "Lips to Lips" (1931) is a caricature of Adamovich and Ivanov milking a wealthy but talentless aspiring writer. See *The Short Stories of Vladimir Nabokov* (New York: Vintage, 1997), 312–24, 652. For a condensed summary of the affair that inspired "Lips to Lips," see Brian Boyd, *Vladimir Nabokov: The Russian Years* (Princeton, N.J.: Princeton University Press, 1990), 373–74.

If only it were possible to write Ivanov off as a hack or even a literary highwayman. When Ivanov's admirer, the pre-Revolutionary literary doyenne Zinaida Gippius, now also in exile, proclaimed Ivanov "the first poet of the diaspora," she may have gone too far (in addition to Marina Tsvetaeva, who was to leave for the Soviet Union, there was also Ivanov's nemesis Vladislav Khodasevich, to name only two logical contenders), but now there could be no doubt that in the course of his career in letters Ivanov evolved into a major twentieth-century Russian poet. If *Gardens* of 1921 and *The Icon Lamp* of 1922 offered little in the way of a new, hitherto unknown poet, the appearance of *Roses* (1931), his first collection of poems to be written exclusively in exile, compelled everyone to talk about him as a principal voice of Russia outside of Russia, which in those days seemed to have been irreversibly swallowed by the Soviet Union. Ivanov's latest poems did not soothe: instead they helped formulate a view on a stark new reality in which loss and absence of hope seemed to demand only those words that were truly needful, with little else accompanying them. *Roses*, therefore, came to epitomize an entire movement in Russian émigré literature called the "Parisian Note." Even though the tragic realization of the imminent end of Russian culture as the world knew it prior to the Revolution was supposed to be expressed by a younger generation of Russian poets abroad, it was Ivanov (and to a certain extent Adamovich, whose poetic output is authentically valuable, if sparse) who gave these eschatological presentiments their most definite embodiment. The main goal of *Petersburg Winters*, Ivanov's largely fictitious—if absorbing—book of memoirs, was to mythologize the real events and actors of the Silver Age to the point of transfiguring them into a legend. In 1938 Ivanov's most controversial prose work, *The Disintegration of the Atom*, was published, and it shocked many a reader with its brazenly cynical exposé of the darkest corners of its lyrical hero's hollowed soul. The turmoil of World War II deprived Ivanov and Odoevtseva—who had once lived comfortably, in contrast to the vast majority of their dispossessed compatriots in exile—of all their worldly possessions. Ivanov's next collection of poems, *A Portrait Without Likeness* (1950), has been called "a miracle of poetic condensation" (Vladimir Markov)[4] and moved closer to the poet's last important topic, his intense contemplation of himself as he came nearer and nearer to the brink of death: *1943–1958. Poems* and *Posthumous Diary* had as their main subject an unsettling chronicle of the author's slow and painful demise. And yet, for all its less-than-uplifting subject matter and its focus on infirmity and death, Ivanov's last verse production became his doleful triumph, a paradoxical affirmation of his art's vitality, not its morbidity.

> *No, it doesn't take much to be born a poet:*
> *But just you try dying as one!*
> (see "No, it doesn't take much to be born a poet," p. 179)

4   See Vladimir Markov, "Georgy Ivanov: Nihilist as Light-Bearer," in *The Bitter Air of Exile*, 161.

Ivanov tried to die a poet, and he succeeded, against all odds and in spite of himself. The end came on August 26, 1958. Ivanov, by then a penniless tenant at a French boardinghouse, was buried in a communal grave. In a gesture indicative of a posthumous reconsideration of the poet's significance, in 1963 Ivanov's remains were relocated to a Russian émigré necropolis in Sainte-Geneviève-des-Bois, where he now rests alongside Andrei Tarkovsky and Rudolf Nureyev.[5]

The poem below is one example of how Ivanov shocked—and continues to shock—his readers by presenting them with a paradoxical mixture of feelings on a given topic. Having little hope to offer his contemporaries, Ivanov was branded a nihilist by the near-sighted amongst them, a claim seemingly supported by the poet himself in such lines as these:

Russia is happiness. Russia is light.
Or, perhaps, there is no Russia at all.

And the sunset did not burn down over the Neva,
And Pushkin did not die on the snow,

And there is no Petersburg, no Kremlin—
Only snow and snow and snow, fields and fields . . .

Snow and snow and snow . . . And the night is long,
And the snow will never melt.

Snow and snow and snow . . . And the night is dark,
And it will never end.

Russia is silence. Russia is dust.
Or, perhaps, Russia is only fear.

A noose, a bullet, the frozen dark
And music that drives you mad.

A noose, a bullet, a forced-labor dawn
Over that for which there is no name in the world.

The author of this poem calls into question a whole nation's most cherished myths—nay, its very existence. Infuriating the faint of heart, Ivanov managed to

5   For detailed accounts of Ivanov's life, see Vadim Kreid, *Georgii Ivanov* (Moscow: Molodaia gvardiia, 2007), and especially Andrei Arieff (Ar'ev), *Zhizn' Georgiia Ivanova: Dokumental'noe povestvovanie* (St. Petersburg: Zhurnal "Zvezda)," 2009.

affirm the paradoxical fact of the continued existence of a country that by all indications had ceased to exist. The more discerning of Ivanov's readers realize that his negation becomes his way of affirming the permanence of the values threatened by the vagaries of time and fate; these readers appreciate the crystalline purity and perfection of the form in which he clothed his most accomplished creations. Ivanov the mature poet shuns superficial effects, instead choosing to concentrate on the hard-won simplicity of his rhymed Russian verse, of which our unrhymed English paraphrases are mere reflections:

> *Mirrors reflect each other,*
> *Mutually distorting their reflections.*
>
> *I believe not in the invincibility of evil,*
> *But only in the unavoidability of defeat.*
>
> *Not in the music that burned my life,*
> *But in the ash left from the burning.*

This poem is characteristic of Ivanov's vintage lyricism. Somber and precise in its expressiveness, it draws an ironic line under a lifelong search for the means of expression uniquely suitable to the task of creating a fitting monument to the poet's many disappointments, be they subjective, intimate, or philosophical. Paradoxically, perhaps, what may be taken for this poem's bitterness, thanks to the degree of its distillation, becomes its redeeming factor, giving us a taste—or rather a foretaste—of the genuineness of Ivanov's lyricism. More is offered below.

Stanislav Shvabrin

РОЗЫ
ROSES

(1931)

Над закатами и розами —
Остальное всё равно —
Над торжественными звёздами
Наше счастье зажжено.

Счастье мучить или мучиться,
Ревновать и забывать.
Счастье нам от Бога данное,
Счастье наше долгожданное,
И другому не бывать.

Всё другое только музыка,
Отраженье, колдовство —
Или синее, холодное,
Бесконечное, бесплодное
Мировое торжество.

1930

Above sunsets and roses,
The rest, it's all the same—
Above stars triumphant
Our happiness enflamed.

Happiness to torture or be tortured,
To be jealous and to forget.
Happiness is given from God,
Our long-awaited happiness,
There is no other.

All the rest is only music,
Reflection, sorcery—
Or blue, cold,
Endless, fruitless
Universal triumph.

1930

Глядя на огонь или дремля
В опьяненьи полусонном —
Слышишь, как летит земля
С бесконечным, лёгким звоном.

Слышишь, как растёт трава,
Как жаз-банд гремит в Париже —
И мутнеющая голова
Опускается всё ниже.

Так и надо. Голову на грудь
Под блаженный шорох моря или сада.
Так и надо — навсегда уснуть,
Больше ничего не надо.

Peering at the fire or drowsing
Intoxicated in half-sleep—
Hear how the earth flies along
With an endless, soft sound.

Hear how the grass grows,
How a jazz band bangs in Paris—
And the mind growing dull
Sinks ever lower.

So it must be. Head on chest
To the blessed rustle of the sea or garden.
So it must be—to fall asleep forever,
Nothing more is needed.

Синий вечер, тихий ветер
И (целуя руки эти)
В небе, розовом до края, —
Догорая, умирая . . .
В небе, розовом до муки,
Плыли птицы или звёзды
И (целуя эти руки)
Было рано или поздно —

В небе, розовом до края,
Тихо кануть в сумрак томный,
Ничего, как жизнь, не зная,
Ничего, как смерть, не помня.

1930

Blue evening, soft wind
And (kissing these hands)
In the sky, rosy to the edge,—
Burning down, dying away . . .
In the sky, rosy to torment,
Birds or stars swam
And (kissing these hands)
It was early or late—

In the sky, rosy to the edge,
Softly sinking into the languid twilight,
Knowing nothing, like life,
Remembering nothing, like death.

1930

Душа черства. И с каждым днём черствей.
— Я гибну. Дай мне руку. Нет ответа.
Ещё я вслушиваюсь в шум ветвей.
Ещё люблю игру теней и света . . .

Да, я ещё живу. Но что мне в том,
Когда я больше не имею власти
Соединить в создании одном
Прекрасного разрозненные части.

My soul is coarse, and coarser with each day.
I'll perish. Give me your hand. No answer.
I still listen in to the sound of branches,
I still love the play of shadow and light . . .

Yes, I'm living still. But what is it for me,
When I no longer have the strength
To unite in a single creation
The disjointed parts of the beautiful.

Не было измены. Только тишина.
Вечная любовь, вечная весна.

Только колыханье синеватых бус,
Только поцелуя солоноватый вкус.

И шумело только о любви моей
Голубое море, словно соловей.

Глубокое море у этих детских ног.
И не было измены — видит Бог.

Только грусть и нежность, нежность вся до дна.
Вечная любовь, вечная весна.

There was no betrayal. Only silence.
Eternal love, eternal spring.

Only the flicking of bluish beads,
Only the salty taste of a kiss.

And the pale blue sea trilled
Like a nightingale, only of my love.

The deep sea at these childish feet.
And God sees—there was no betrayal.

Only sadness and tenderness, tenderness to the bottom.
Eternal love, eternal spring.

Напрасно пролита кровь,
И грусть, и верность напрасна—
Мой ангел, моя любовь,
И всё-таки жизнь прекрасна.

Деревья легко шумят,
И чайки кружат над нами,
Огромный морской закат
Бросает косое пламя . . .

Blood is spilled in vain,
And sadness, and loyalty are no use—
Yet, my angel, my love,
Life is still wondrous.

The trees lightly rustle,
And gulls circle above us,
A huge ocean sunset
Casts down a slanting flame . . .

Перед тем, как умереть,
Надо же глаза закрыть.
Перед тем, как замолчать,
Надо же поговорить.

Звёзды разбивают лёд.
Призраки встают со дна—
Слишком быстро настаёт
Слишком нежная весна.

И касаясь торжества,
Превращаясь в торжество,
Рассыпаются слова
И не значат ничего.

1930

Before one is to die,
One's got to close one's eyes.
Before one is to fall silent,
One's got to talk a bit.

The stars break the ice.
Ghosts stand up from the bottom—
The too-tender springtime
Too quickly comes to be.

Touching on triumph,
Transforming into triumph,
Words spill out
And mean nothing.

1930

Я слышу — история и человечество,
Я слышу — изгнание или отечество.

Я в книгах читаю — добро, лицемерие,
Надежда, отчаянье, вера, неверие.

Я вижу огромное, страшное, нежное,
Насквозь ледяное, навек безнадежное.

И вижу беспамятство или мучение,
Где всё, навсегда, потеряло значение.

И вижу, вне времени и расстояния, —
Над бедной землёй неземное сияние.

1930

I hear: "history and mankind,"
I hear: "exile or homeland."

In books I read: "the good, the hypocrisy,
Hope, despair, faith, lack of faith."

I see the huge, the horrible, the tender,
The frozen through, the eternally hopeless.

I see the delirium or the suffering,
Where everything has forever lost meaning.

I see, beyond time and space,
An unearthly radiance above our poor Earth.

1930

Тёплый ветер веет с юга,
Умирает человек.
Это вьюга, это вьюга,
Это вьюга крутит снег.

«Пожалей меня, подруга,
Так ужасно умирать!»
Только ветер веет с юга,
Да и слов не разобрать.

—Тот блажен, кто умирает,
Тот блажен, кто обречен,
В миг, когда он всё теряет,
Всё приобретает он.

«Пожалей меня, подруга!»
И уже ни капли сил.

Тёплый ветер веет с юга,
С белых ка́мней и могил.
Заметает быстро вьюга
Всё, что в мире ты любил.

1930

A warm wind wafts from the south,
A man is dying.
It's a storm, a snowstorm,
A snowstorm swirls the snow.

"Pity me, my darling,
It's so horrible to die!"
Only the wind wafts from the south,
And there's no making out the words.

Blessed is he who dies,
Blessed is he who is doomed,
In that instant when he loses all,
He gains everything.

"Pity me, my darling!"
I've no longer a drop of strength.

A warm wind wafts from the south,
From the white headstones and the graves.
The storm quickly wipes out
All that you loved in the world.

1930

Балтийское море дымилось
И словно рвалось на закат,
Балтийское солнце садилось
За синий и дальний Кронштадт.

И так широко освещало
Тревожное море в дыму,
Как будто ещё обещало
Какое-то счастье ему.

The Baltic Sea was smoking
And tore apart, becoming sunset;
The Baltic sun was setting
Beyond blue, faraway Kronstadt.

And the sun so broadly lit up
The troubled sea in the smoke,
As if still promising the city
Some kind of happiness.

Чёрная кровь из открытых жил—
И ангел, как птица, крылья сложил . . .

Это было на слабом, весеннем льду
В девятьсот двадцатом году.

Дай мне руку, иначе я упаду—
Так скользко на этом льду.

Над широкой Невой догорал закат.
Цепенели дворцы, чернели мосты—

Это было тысячу лет назад,
Так давно, что забыла ты.

Black blood from opened veins—
And an angel, like a bird, folded his wings . . .

It was on the weak, spring ice
In the year nineteen-hundred and twenty.

Give me your hand, or else I'll fall,
It's so slippery on this ice.

The sunset faded over the broad Neva.
The palaces froze, the bridges stood dark—

It was a thousand years past,
So long ago that you've forgotten.

Как в Грецию Байрон, о, без сожаленья,
Сквозь звёзды и розы, и тьму,
На голос бессмысленно-сладкого пенья . . .
　　—И ты не поможешь ему.

Сквозь звёзды, которые снятся влюблённым,
И небо, где нет ничего,
В холодную полночь—платком надушённым . . .
　　—И ты не удержишь его.

На голос бессмысленно-сладкого пенья,
Как Байрон за бледным огнём,
Сквозь полночь и розы, о, без сожаленья . . .
　　—И ты позабудешь о нём.

Like Byron to Greece, O, without regret,
Through stars, and roses, and darkness,
Following a voice of senselessly sweet singing . . .
        —And you have no way of helping him.

Through stars dreamt by lovers,
And the sky, where there is nothing,
Into cold midnight—a perfumed handkerchief . . .
        —And you have no way of holding him back.

Following a voice of senselessly sweet singing,
Like Byron in pursuit of a pale fire,
Through midnight and roses, O, without regret . . .
        —And you have no way of remembering him.

Это только синий ладан,
Это только сон во сне,
Звёзды над пустынным садом,
Розы на твоём окне.

Это то, что в мире этом
Называется весной,
Тишиной, прохладным светом
Над прохладной глубиной.

Взмахи чёрных вёсел шире,
Чище сумрак голубой—
Это то, что в этом мире
Называется судьбой.

То, что ничего не значит
И не знает ни о чем—
Только тёплым морем плачет,
Только парусом маячит
Над обветренным плечом.

1930

This is only blue incense,
This is only a dream within a dream,
Stars over a deserted garden,
Roses on your window.

This is what in this world
Is called Spring,
Silence, with a cool light
Above the cool deep.

Wider is the pull of dark oars,
Purer is the pale blue twilight—
This is what in this world
Is called Fate.

What has no meaning
And knows of nothing—
Only weeping as the warm sea,
Only looming as a sail
Above your wind-whipped shoulder.

1930

В сумраке счастья неверного
Смутно горит торжество.
Нет ничего достоверного
В синем сияньи его.
В пропасти холода нежного
Нет ничего неизбежного,
Вечного нет ничего.

Сердце твоё опечалили
Небо, весна и вода.
Лёгкие тучи растаяли,
Лёгкая встала звезда.
Лёгкие лодки отчалили
В синюю даль навсегда.

1930

In the twilight of unfaithful happiness
Dim triumph burns.
There is nothing certain
In its blue radiance.
In the abyss of tender cold
There is nothing unavoidable,
Nothing eternal.

They have saddened your heart
The sky, the spring, and the water.
Light clouds melted away,
A light star arose.
Light boats set sail
Into the blue distance, forever.

1930

В комнате твоей
Слышен шум ветвей
И глядит туда
Белая звезда.
Плачет соловей
За твоим окном,
И светло, как днём,
В комнате твоей.

Только тишина,
Только синий лёд,
И навеки дна
Не достанет лот.
Самый зоркий глаз
Не увидит дна,
Самый чуткий слух
Не услышит час —
Где летит судьба,
Тишина, весна
Одного из двух,
Одного из нас.

1930

In your room
The sound of branches,
And a white star
Peers into it.
A nightingale is crying
Outside your window,
It is bright, like day
In your room.

Only silence,
Only blue ice,
No sounding will ever
Reach the bottom.
The most penetrating eye
Will not see the bottom,
The most sensitive ear
Will not hear the hour—
Where fate flies,
Silence, spring
One or the other,
One of us.

1930

Увяданьем еле тронут
Мир печальный и прекрасный,
Паруса плывут и тонут.
Голоса зовут и гаснут.

Как звезда—фонарь качает.
Без следа—в туман разлуки.
Навсегда?—не отвечает,
Лишь протягивает руки—

Ближе к снегу, к белой пене,
Ближе к звёздам, ближе к дому . . .

. . . И растут ночные тени,
И скользят ночные тени
По лицу уже чужому.

1930

Barely touched by decay
This sad, this marvelous world—
Sails sail and drown.
Voices call and fade away.

Like a star—the lantern rocks.
Without a trace—into the mist of separation.
Forever?—doesn't say a word,
Hands reach out, that's all—

Closer to the snow, to the white foam,
Closer to the stars, closer to home . . .

. . . And evening shadows grow,
And evening shadows slide
Along a face, already strange.

1930

Прислушайся к дальнему пенью
Эоловой арфы нежней—
То море широкою тенью
Ложится у серых камней.

И голос летит из тумана:
— Я всё потерял и забыл,
Печальная дочь океана,
Зачем я тебя полюбил.

Give ear to the distant singing
More tender than the Aeolian harp:
It is the sea, like a wide shade,
Coming to rest by the gray rocks.

And a voice flies out from the mist:
—I've lost all and forgotten,
Sad daughter of the sea,
Why did I fall in love with you . . .

Начало небо меняться,
Медленно месяц проплыл,
Словно быстрее подняться
У него не было сил.

И розоватые звёзды
На розоватой дали
Сквозь холодеющий воздух
Ярче блеснуть не могли.

И погасить их не смела,
И не могла им помочь,
Только тревожно шумела
Чёрными ветками ночь.

1930

The sky began to change,
The crescent moon flowed slowly past,
As if it had no strength
To raise itself faster.

And the roseate stars
In the rose-hued distance
Through the cooling air
Could not shine brighter.

And she didn't dare to put them out,
And she couldn't help them;
Only a night filled with fearful sound,
Black branches waving.

1930

Когда-нибудь и где-нибудь.
Не всё ль равно?
Но розы упадут на грудь,
Звезда блеснёт в окно
Когда-нибудь...

Летит зелёная звезда
Сквозь тишину.
Летит зелёная звезда,
Как ласточка к окну —
В счастливый дом.

И чьё-то сердце навсегда
Остановилось в нём.

Sometime and somewhere,
Does it really matter?
But roses will fall on your chest,
A star will gleam in the window
Sometime . . .

A green star flies
Through the silence.
A green star flies—
Like a swallow to the window—
To a happy home.

And someone's heart
Stopped there, forever.

Злой и грустной полоской рассвета,
Угольком в догоревшей золе,
Журавлём перелётным на этой
Злой и грустной земле . . .

Даже больше—кому это надо—
Просиять сквозь холодную тьму . . .
И деревья пустынного сада
Широко шелестят—«Никому».

Like a bitter, sad streak of daybreak,
Like an ember among burnt ashes,
Like a migrant crane on this
Bitter and sad earth . . .

Even more—who needs it anyway?—
To blaze through cold darkness . . .
And the trees of a deserted garden
Rustle open wide: "No one."

Закроешь глаза на мгновенье
И вместе с прохладой вдохнёшь
Какое-то дальнее пенье,
Какую-то смутную дрожь.

И нет ни России, ни мира,
И нет ни любви, ни обид—
По синему царству эфира
Свободное сердце летит.

Close your eyes for a moment
And with the cool air breathe in
Some sort of far-off singing,
Some sort of troubled shiver.

And there is no Russia, no universe,
And no love, and no hurt—
The free heart flies on
Through a blue realm of ether.

Хорошо, что нет Царя.
Хорошо, что нет России.
Хорошо, что Бога нет.

Только жёлтая заря,
Только звёзды ледяные,
Только миллионы лет.

Хорошо — что никого,
Хорошо — что ничего,
Так черно и так мертво,

Что мертвее быть не может
И чернее не бывать,
Что никто нам не поможет
И не надо помогать.

1930

Nice—there is no Tsar.
Nice—there is no Russia.
Nice—there is no God.

Only the yellow dawn,
Only the icy stars,
Only millions of years.

Nice—there is no one,
Nice—there is no thing,
So dark, and so dead,

That deader cannot be
And darker cannot happen,
That no one will help us
And no help is needed.

1930

В тринадцатом году, ещё не понимая,
Что будет с нами, что нас ждёт,—
Шампанского бокалы подымая,
Мы весело встречали—Новый Год.

Как мы состарились! Проходят годы,
Проходят годы—их не замечаем мы . . .
Но этот воздух смерти и свободы,
И розы, и вино, и счастье той зимы
Никто не позабыл, о, я уверен . . .

Должно быть, сквозь свинцовый мрак,
На мир, что навсегда потерян,
Глаза умерших смотрят так.

In 1913, not understanding yet
What would become of us, what awaited us,
Merrily we rang in the New Year,
Raising glasses of champagne.

How we have aged! The years pass,
The years pass, and we do not notice them.
But that air of death and freedom,
And the roses, wine, and happiness of that winter
No one forgot, of that I'm quite sure.

It must be thus that the eyes of the dead
Look through the leaden gloom,
At a world lost forever.

Россия, Россия «рабоче-крестьянская» —
И как не отчаяться! —
Едва началось твое счастье цыганское
И вот уж кончается.

Деревни голодные, степи бесплодные . . .
И лёд твой не тронется —
Едва поднялось твоё солнце холодное
И вот уже клонится.

1930

Russia, the Russia of "workers and peasants"—
How can one not despair!
Your gypsy happiness had hardly begun
And here it is already ending.

Hungry villages, barren steppe lands . . .
And your ice will not budge—
Your cold sun had hardly risen
And here it is already setting.

1930

Холодно бродить по свету,
Холодней лежать в гробу.
Помни это, помни это,
Не кляни свою судьбу.

Ты ещё читаешь Блока,
Ты ещё глядишь в окно,
Ты ещё не знаешь срока—
Всё неясно, всё жестоко,
Всё навек обречено.

И, конечно, жизнь прекрасна,
И, конечно, смерть страшна,
Отвратительна, ужасна,
Но всему одна цена.

Помни это, помни это
—Каплю жизни, каплю света . . .

«Донна Анна! Нет ответа.
Анна, Анна! Тишина».

1930

How cold it is to roam the world,
Colder still to lie in the grave.
Remember this, remember this,
Do not curse your fate.

You still read Blok,
You still look out the window,
You still don't know how long—
All is unclear, all is cruel,
Everything is doomed forever.

And of course, life is wonderful,
And of course, death is terrible,
Repulsive, horrible,
But the price is the same for all.

Remember this, remember this
—A drop of life, a drop of light . . .

"Donna Anna!" No answer.
"Anna, Anna!" Silence.

1930

По улицам рассеянно мы бродим,
На женщин смотрим и в кафе сидим,
Но настоящих слов мы не находим,
А приблизительных мы больше не хотим.

И что же делать? В Петербург вернуться?
Влюбиться? Или Опера́ взорвать?
Иль просто — лечь в холодную кровать,
Закрыть глаза и больше не проснуться . . .

Absent-minded, we wander the streets,
Stare at women and sit in cafes,
But true words we cannot find,
And imprecise ones we no longer want.

And what are we to do? Return to Petersburg?
Fall in love? Blow up the Opéra?
Or simply—lie down in a cold bed,
Close your eyes and wake no more . . .

Для чего, как на двери небесного рая,
Нам на это прекрасное небо смотреть,
Каждый миг умирая и вновь воскресая
Для того, чтобы вновь умереть.

Для чего этот лёгкий торжественный воздух
Голубой средиземной зимы
Обещает, что где-то — быть может, на звёздах —
Будем счастливы мы.

Утомительный день утомительно прожит,
Голова тяжела, и над ней
Розовеет закат — о, последний, быть может, —
Всё нежней, и нежней, и нежней . . .

Why, as at the gates of heavenly paradise,
Should we be looking at this splendid sky,
Dying every instant, resurrected again
In order once again to die.

Why this light, triumphant air
A sky-blue Mediterranean winter
Promises that somewhere—perhaps, on stars—
We will be happy.

A wearisome day wearily lived through,
The head is heavy, and above
The sunset—perhaps the last—grows rosy
Tender, more tender, ever more tender . . .

Страсть? А если нет и страсти?
Власть? А если нет и власти
Даже над самим собой?

Что же делать мне с тобой.

Только не гляди на звёзды,
Не грусти и не влюбляйся,
Не читай стихов певучих
И за счастье не цепляйся—

Счастья нет, мой бедный друг.

Счастье выпало из рук,
Камнем в море утонуло,
Рыбкой золотой плеснуло,
Льдинкой уплыло на юг.

Счастье нет, и мы не дети.
Вот и надо выбирать—
Или жить, как все на свете,
Или умирать.

1930

Passion? What if there isn't any passion?
Power? What if there isn't any power
Even over oneself?

What can I do with you?

Just don't look at the stars,
Do not be sad and do not fall in love,
Do not read lilting poems
And do not go running after happiness—

There is no happiness, my poor friend.

Happiness fell from our hands,
And sank like a stone in the sea,
Splashed like a goldfish,
Drifted southward like a chip of ice.

There is no happiness, and we are not children.
So a choice must be made—
Either live like everyone else in the world,
Or die.

1930

Как грустно и всё же как хочется жить,
А в воздухе пахнет весной.
И вновь мы готовы за счастье платить
Какою угодно ценой.

И люди кричат, экипажи летят,
Сверкает огнями Конкорд—
И розовый, нежный, парижский закат
Широкою тенью простёрт.

How sad—and still one so wants to live,
The smell of spring is in the air.
And again we are ready to pay
For happiness, whatever the price.

And people shout, carriages fly along,
Place de la Concorde sparkles with lights—
And a rosy, tender Paris sunset
Spreads out like a broad shadow.

Так тихо гаснул этот день. Едва
Блеснула медью чешуя канала,
Сухая, пожелтевшая листва
Предсмертным шорохом затрепетала.

Мы плыли в узкой лодке по волнам,
Нам было грустно, как всегда влюблённым,
И этот бледно-синий вечер нам
Казался существом одушевлённым.

Как будто говорил он: я не жду
Ни счастия, ни солнечного света—
На этот бедный лоб немного льду,
Немного жалости на сердце это.

This day faded so quietly. The burnished
Ripple-scales of the canal barely sparkled,
The dry, yellowed foliage
Trembled with a dying rustle.

We sailed the waves in a narrow boat,
We were sad, as those in love are always,
And this pale-blue evening seemed
To us to be an animated being.

It was as if it had said: I do not expect
Either happiness, or sunshine—
Only a little ice on this poor brow,
Only a little pity for this heart.

Грустно, друг. Всё слаще, всё нежнее
Ветер с моря. Слабый звёздный свет.
Грустно, друг. И тем ещё грустнее,
Что надежды больше нет.

Это уж не романтизм. Какая
Там Шотландия! Взгляни: горит
Между чёрных лип звезда большая
И о смерти говорит.

Пахнет розами. Спокойной ночи.
Ветер с моря, руки на груди.
И в последний раз в пустые очи
Звёзд бессмертных — погляди.

It is sad, my friend. The sea breeze ever
Sweet and more tender. The weak starlight.
It is sad, my friend. And sadder still
That there is no longer hope.

It's not Romanticism anymore. Who cares
About Scotland anyway! Look: a large star
Burns among dark linden trees
And it speaks of death.

The fragrance of roses. Good night!
The sea breeze, hands crossed on breast.
Look now for the last time into
The empty eyes of immortal stars.

Не спится мне. Зажечь свечу?
Да только спичек нет.
Весь мир молчит, и я молчу,
Гляжу на лунный свет.

И думаю: как много глаз
В такой же тишине.
В такой же тихий, ясный час
Устремлено к луне.

Как скучно ей, должно быть, плыть
Над головой у нас,
Чужие окна серебрить
И видеть столько глаз.

Сто лет вперёд, сто лет назад,
А в мире всё одно—
Собаки лают, да глядят
Мечтатели в окно.

I can't sleep. Light a candle?
Only there are no matches.
The whole world is silent, and I am silent,
I gaze at the lunar light.

And think: how many eyes
In just this same silence,
At such a quiet, clear hour
Are trained on the moon.

How tedious it must be to swim
Above our heads,
To coat strange windows with silver
And to see so many eyes.

A century ahead, a century back,
But in the world all is the same—
Dogs bark, and dreamers
Gaze out the window.

Как лёд наше бедное счастье растает,
Растает как лёд, словно камень утонет,
Держи, если можешь, — оно улетает,
Оно улетит, и никто не догонит.

Our meager happiness melts like ice,
Melts like ice and sinks like a stone,
Hang on, if you can—it's flying away,
It will fly off, and no one will catch it.

Январский день. На берегу Невы
Несётся ветер, разрушеньем вея.
Где Олечка Судейкина, увы!
Ахматова, Паллада, Саломея?
Все, кто блистал в тринадцатом году —
Лишь призраки на петебургском льду.

Вновь соловьи засвищут в тополях,
И на закате, в Павловске иль Царском,
Пройдёт другая дама в соболях,
Другой влюблённый в ментике гусарском . . .
Но Всеволода Князева они
Не вспомнят в дорогой ему тени.

January day, at the Neva's shore
The wind blows hard, portending ruin.
Where is Olechka Sudeikina, alas,
Akhmatova, Pallada, Salomea?
All those who shone in nineteen-thirteen—
They are now only phantoms on the Petersburg ice.

The nightingales will trill once again in the poplars,
In Pavlovsk or Tsarskoe at sunset
A different woman will pass by in her sables,
A different man-in-love in his hussar's pelisse.
But they won't recall Vsevolod Kniazev
In that shade he loved so dearly.

Синеватое облако
(Холодок у виска)
Синеватое облако
И ещё облака . . .

И старинная яблоня
(Может быть, подождать?)
Простодушная яблоня
Зацветает опять.

Всё какое-то русское—
(Улыбнись и нажми!)
Это облако узкое,
Словно лодка с детьми.

И особенно синяя
(С первым боем часов . . .)
Безнадежная линия
Бесконечных лесов.

A bluish cloud
(A chill at my temple)
A bluish cloud
And still more clouds . . .

And an ancient apple tree
(Perhaps I should wait awhile?)
The simple-hearted apple tree
Bursting into bloom again.

It all looks so Russian—
(Smile and pull it!)
This narrow cloud
Just like a small boat with children.

And so astonishingly blue
(With the first strike of the clock . . .)
That hopeless line
Of endless forests.

В глубине, на самом дне сознанья,
Как на дне колодца — самом дне —
Отблеск нестерпимого сиянья
Пролетает иногда во мне.

Боже! И глаза я закрываю
От невыносимого огня.
Падаю в него . . .
                        и понимаю,
Что глядят соседи по трамваю
Страшными глазами на меня.

In the depths, at the very bottom of consciousness,
As if at the bottom of a well—the very bottom—
A reflection of unbearable radiance
Flies by sometimes within me.

God! I close my eyes
Against the unendurable fire.
I sink into it . . .

                                only to realize
That my neighbors in the tram
Are staring at me with horrified eyes.

Утро было как утро. Нам было довольно приятно.
Чашки чёрного кофе были лилово-черны,
Скатерть ярко-бела, и на скатерти рюмки и пятна.

Утро было как утро. Конечно, мы были пьяны.
Англичане с соседнего столика что-то мычали—
Что-то о испытаньях великой союзной страны.

Кто-то сел за рояль и запел, и кого-то качали . . .
Утро было как утро—розы дождливой весны
Плыли в широком окне, ледяном океане печали.

A morning like any other. We were quite content.
The cups of black coffee were violet black,
A bright-white tablecloth, shot glasses, stains.

A morning like any other. Yes, we were drunk.
The Englishmen at the next table mumbled something,
Something about the ordeals of a great ally nation.

Someone sat at the piano and sang, someone got tossed into the air . . .
A morning like any other—roses of a rainy spring
Swam in the wide window, in an icy ocean of grief.

Медленно и неуверенно
Месяц встаёт над землёй.
Чёрные ветки качаются,
Пахнет весной и травой.

И отражается в озере,
И холодеет на дне
Небо, слегка декадентское,
В бледно-зелёном огне.

Всё в этом мире по-прежнему.
Месяц встаёт, как вставал,
Пушкин именье закладывал
Или жену ревновал.

И ничего не исправила,
Не помогла ничему,
Смутная, чудная музыка,
Слышная только ему.

Slowly and timidly
The moon rises over the earth.
Dark branches sway to and fro,
The air is redolent of spring and grass.

And, reflected in the lake,
The sky grows cold at the bottom,
And, slightly decadent,
In its pale-green flame.

Everything in this world is as before.
The moon rises as it always rose,
Pushkin mortgaged his estate
Or was jealous of his wife.

And nothing was put right,
Was of no help for anything,
That dim, magical music,
Audible to him alone.

От синих звёзд, которым дела нет
До глаз, на них глядящих с упованьем,
От вечных звёзд — ложится синий свет
Над сумрачным земным существованьем.

И сердце беспокоится. И в нём —
О, никому на свете незаметный —
Вдруг чудным загорается огнём
Навстречу звёздному лучу — ответный.

И надо всём мне в мире дорогим
Он холодно скользит к границе мира,
Чтобы скреститься там с лучом другим,
Как золотая тонкая рапира.

From blue stars, who are indifferent to
Eyes that peer at them with hope,
From eternal stars—a blue light spreads
Over the earth's twilight existence.

And the heart aches. And in it—
O, unnoticed by anyone in the world—
Suddenly a wondrous flame ignites
To meet the starry ray—in answer.

Above all that is dear to me in the world
It slides coldly to the edge of the world,
In order to cross there with another ray,
Like a thin golden rapier.

Даль грустна, ясна, холодна, темна,
Холодна, ясна, грустна.

Эта грусть, которая звёзд полна,
Эта грусть и есть весна.

Голубеет лес, чернеет мост,
Вечер тих и полон звёзд.

И кому страшна о смерти весть,
Та, что в этой нежности есть?

И кому нужна та, что так нежна,
Что нежнее всего — весна?

The melancholy distance, clear, cold, and dark—
Cold, clear, and sad.

This sadness, filled with stars,
This sadness is indeed the spring.

The forest grows blue, the bridge darkens,
The evening is quiet and filled with stars.

And who is terrified by the news of death,
The one lodged in this tenderness?

And who needs what is so tender,
Most tender of all—spring?

Все розы, которые в мире цвели,
И все соловьи, и все журавли,

И в чёрном гробу восковая рука,
И все паруса, и все облака,

И все корабли, и все имена,
И эта, забытая Богом, страна!

Так чёрные ангелы медленно падали в мрак,
Так чёрною тенью Титаник клонился ко дну,

Так сердце твоё оборвётся когда-нибудь — так
Сквозь розы и ночь, снега и весну . . .

All the roses that bloomed in the world,
And all the nightingales, and all the cranes,

And in a dark coffin a waxen hand,
And all the sails, and all the clouds,

And all the ships, and all the names,
And this land, forgotten by God!

This way black angels slowly fell into the dark,
This way *Titanic's* dark shadow angled toward the bottom,

This way your heart will come undone one day—this way
Through roses, night, snows, and spring . . .

from

ОТПЛЫТИЕ НА ОСТРОВ ЦИТЕРУ

Избранные стихи

EMBARKATION FOR
THE ISLAND OF CYTHERA

Selected Poems

1916–1936

(1937)

О, высок, весна, высок твой синий терем,
Твой душистый клевер полевой.
О, далёк твой путь за звёздами на север,
Снежный ветер, белый веер твой.

Вьётся голубок. Надежда улетает.
Катится клубок . . . О, как земля мала.
О, глубок твой снег, и никогда не тает.
Слишком мало на земле тепла.

O, spring, high, high your castle blue,
Your fragrant field of clover.
O, your path far north beyond the stars
The snowy wind, your fan of white.

A dove wafts by. Hope flies away.
A ball of yarn rolls on. O, how small the world.
O, your snow is deep, and never melts.
There's too little warmth in the world.

Это месяц плывёт по эфиру,
Это лодка скользит по волнам,
Это жизнь приближается к миру,
Это смерть улыбается нам.
Обрывается лодка с причала
И уносит, уносит её . . .
Это детство и счастье сначала,
Это детство и счастье твоё.

Да, — и то, что зовётся любовью,
Да, — и то, что надеждой звалось,
Да, — и то, что дымящейся кровью
На сияющий снег пролилось.
. . . Ветки сосен — они шелестели:
«Милый друг, погоди, погоди . . .»
Это призрак стоит у постели
И цветы прижимает к груди.

Приближается звёздная вечность,
Рассыпается пылью гранит,
Бесконечность, одна бесконечность
В леденеющем мире звенит.
Это музыка миру прощает
То, что жизнь никогда не простит.
Это музыка путь освещает,
Где погибшее счастье летит.

The moon swims in the ether,
The boat slides along the waves,
Life draws close to the world,
Death smiles at us.
The boat tears away from its mooring
And is carried, carried away . . .
From the beginning, childhood and happiness,
Your childhood and your happiness.

Yes, and what is called love,
Yes, and what used to be called hope,
Yes, and what was spilled with smoking blood
Onto the dazzling snow.
Pine branches rustled:
"Dear friend, wait, just wait . . ."
A ghost stands by the bed
Pressing flowers to its chest.

Starry eternity approaches,
Granite crumbles to dust,
Infinity, endless infinity
Resounds in a world turned ice.
Music forgives the world
What life will never forgive.
Music illuminates the path
Where lost happiness flies on.

Россия счастие. Россия свет.
А, может быть, России вовсе нет.

И над Невой закат не догорал,
И Пушкин на снегу не умирал,

И нет ни Петербурга, ни Кремля —
Одни снега, снега, снега, поля, поля . . .

Снега, снега, снега . . . А ночь долга,
И не растают никогда снега.

Снега, снега, снега . . . А ночь темна,
И никогда не кончится она.

Россия тишина. Россия прах.
А, может быть, Россия — только страх.

Верёвка, пуля, ледяная тьма
И музыка, сводящая с ума.

Верёвка, пуля, каторжный рассвет
Над тем, чему названья в мире нет.

Russia is happiness. Russia is light.
Or, perhaps, there is no Russia at all.

And the sunset did not burn down over the Neva,
And Pushkin did not die on the snow,

And there is no Petersburg, no Kremlin—
Only snow and snow and snow, fields and fields . . .

Snow and snow and snow . . . And the night is long,
And the snow will never melt.

Snow and snow and snow . . . And the night is dark,
And it will never end.

Russia is silence. Russia is dust.
Or, perhaps, Russia is only fear.

A noose, a bullet, the frozen dark
And music that drives you mad.

A noose, a bullet, a forced-labor dawn
Over that for which there is no name in the world.

Только всего—простодушный напев,
Только всего—умирающий звук,
Только свеча, нагорев, догорев . . .
Только. И падает скрипка из рук.

Падает песня в предвечную тьму,
Падает мёртвая скрипка за ней . . .

И, неподвластна уже никому,
В тысячу раз тяжелей и нежней,
Слаще и горестней в тысячу раз,
Тысячью звёзд, что на небе горит,
Тысячью слёз из растерянных глаз—

Чудное эхо её повторит.

Just that—a simple-hearted melody,
Just that—a dying sound,
Just a candle, burnt down, burnt out . . .
Just. And a violin falls from the hands.

A song falls into primordial darkness,
A dead violin falls in its wake . . .

And, now independent of anyone,
A thousand times heavier and more tender,
A thousand times sweeter and more sorrowful,
A thousand stars that burn in heaven,
A thousand tears from eyes overcome—

A marvelous echo will repeat the melody.

Слово за словом, строка за строкой —
Все о тебе ослабевшей рукой.

Розы и жалобы — все о тебе.
Полночь. Сиянье. Покорность судьбе.

Полночь. Сиянье. Ты в мире одна.
Ты тишина, ты заря, ты весна.

И холодна ты, как вечный покой . . .
Слово за словом, строка за строкой,

Капля за каплей — кровь и вода —
В синюю вечность твою навсегда.

Word after word, line after line—
All about you, with this weakened hand.

Roses and laments—all about you.
Midnight. Radiance. Resignation to fate.

Midnight. Radiance. You are alone in the world.
You are silence, you are dawn, you are spring.

And you are cold, like eternal peace . . .
Word after word, line after line,

Drop after drop—blood and water—
Into your blue eternity, forever.

Музыка мне больше не нужна.
Музыка мне больше не слышна.

Пусть себе, как чёрная стена,
К звёздам подымается она,

Пусть себе, как чёрная волна,
Глухо рассыпается она.

Ничего не может изменить
И не может ничему помочь

То, что только плачет, и звенит,
И туманит, и уходит в ночь . . .

Music is no longer needed by me.
Music is no longer heard by me.

Let it, like a black wall,
Rise to the stars,

Let it, like a black wave,
Dully crumble down.

Nothing can change
And nothing can help—

That which only cries, and rings out,
And mists, and exits into the night . . .

Звёзды синеют. Деревья качаются.
Вечер как вечер. Зима как зима.
Всё прощено. Ничего не прощается.
Музыка. Тьма.

Все мы герои и все мы изменники,
Всем, одинаково, верим словам.
Что ж, дорогие мои современники,
Весело вам?

Stars shine deep blue. Trees sway.
Evening like evening. Winter like winter.
All is forgiven. Nothing can be forgiven.
Music. Darkness.

We are all heroes and we are all betrayers,
We believe all words, equally.
Well then, my dear contemporaries,
Having a good time?

Ни светлым именем богов,
Ни тёмным именем природы!
. . . Ещё у этих берегов
Шумят деревья, плещут воды . . .

Мир оплывает, как свеча,
И пламя пальцы обжигает.
Бессмертной музыкой звуча,
Он ширится и погибает.
И тьма—уже не тьма, а свет,
И да—уже не да, а нет.

. . . И не восстанут из гробов
И не вернут былой свободы—
Ни светлым именем богов,
Ни тёмным именем природы!

Она прекрасна, эта мгла.
Она похожа на сиянье.
Добра и зла, добра и зла
В ней неразрывное слиянье.
Добра и зла, добра и зла
Смысл, раскалённый добела.

Neither by the hallowed name of the gods,
Nor by the dark name of nature!
. . . Still trees sway, and waters splash
Along these shores . . .

The world gutters like a candle,
And the flame singes the fingers.
It expands and perishes,
Sounding out with immortal music.
And the dark—already not dark, but light,
And yes—already not yes, but no.

They will not arise from their tombs,
They will not be restored their bygone freedom—
Neither by the hallowed name of the gods,
Nor by the dark name of nature!

It is lovely, this gloaming.
It resembles a radiance.
Of good and evil—good and evil—
In it their irreversible fusion.
Of good and evil—good and evil—
Their essence heated white-hot.

Только звёзды. Только синий воздух,
Синий, вечный, ледяной.
Синий, грозный, сине-звёздный
Над тобой и надо мной.

Тише, тише. За полярным кругом
Спят, не разнимая рук,
С верным другом, с неразлучным другом,
С мёртвым другом, мёртвый друг.

Им спокойно вместе, им блаженно рядом . . .
Тише, тише. Не дыши.
Это только звёзды над пустынным садом,
Только синий свет твоей души.

Only stars, only blue air—
Blue, eternal, made of ice.
Blue, grand, blue-star-hued
Over you and over me.

Quiet, quiet. Beyond the Polar Circle
They sleep, hand in hand,
A true friend with an inseparable friend,
With a dead friend—a dead friend.

They are at peace, together blessed . . .
Quiet, quiet. Don't breathe.
These are only stars above an empty garden,
Only the blue light of your soul.

Сиянье. В двенадцать часов по ночам,
Из гроба.
Всё—тёмные розы по детским плечам.
И нежность, и злоба.

И верность. О, верность верна!
Шампанское взоры туманит . . .
И музыка. Только она
Одна не обманет.

О, всё это шорох ночных голосов,
О, всё это было когда-то—
Над синими далями русских лесов
В торжественной грусти заката . . .
Сиянье. Сиянье. Двенадцать часов.
Расплата.

The radiance. At midnight every night,
From the grave.
Everything—the dark roses on children's shoulders.
And tenderness, and spite.

And loyalty. O, loyalty true!
Champagne clouds glances . . .
And music. It alone
Will not deceive.

O, this is all the rustle of voices in the night,
O, this was all long ago—
Above the blue expanses of Russian forests
In the triumphant sadness of the sunset . . .
The radiance. The radiance. Midnight.
The reckoning.

Замело тебя, счастье, снегами,
Унесло на столетья назад,
Затоптало тебя сапогами
Отступающих в вечность солдат.

Только в сумраке Нового Года
Белой музыки бьётся крыло:
— Я надежда, я жизнь, я свобода.
Но снегами меня замело.

Happiness, the snows have covered you,
Carried you centuries back,
Stomped on you with the boots
Of soldiers retreating into eternity.

Only the wing of white music
Flails in the twilight of the New Year:
—I am hope, I am life, I am freedom.
But the snows have covered me.

О, душа моя, могло ли быть иначе.
Разве ты ждала, что жизнь тебя простит?
Это только в сказках: Золушка заплачет,
Добрый лес зашелестит . . .

Всё-таки, душа, не будь неблагодарной,
Всё-таки не плачь . . .
                Над тёмным миром зла
Высоко сиял венец звезды полярной,
И жестокой, чистой, грозной, лучезарной
Смерть твоя была.

O, my soul, could it have been different?
Did you really expect that life would forgive you?
That's all in fairy tales: Cinderella will cry,
The good forest will rustle . . .

All the same, my soul, don't be ungrateful,
All the same, don't cry . . .
        Over the dark world of evil
The wreath of the Polar Star shone on high,
And cruel, pure, terrible, and resplendent
Was your death.

Так иль этак. Так иль этак.
Всё равно. Всё решено
Колыханьем чёрных веток
Сквозь морозное окно.

Годы долгие решалась,
А задача так проста.
Нежность под ноги бросалась,
Суетилась суета.

Всё равно. Качнулись ветки
Снежным ветром по судьбе.
Слёзы, медленны и едки,
Льются сами по себе.

Но тому, кто тихо плачет,
Молча стоя у окна,
Ничего уже не значит,
Что задача решена.

This way or that, this way or that.
All the same, all decided
By the flickering of dark branches
Through a frosted window.

It took years of solving—
Yet the problem is so simple.
Tenderness threw itself underfoot,
Vanity made a fuss.

All the same, branches swayed
To the snowy wind borne across my fate.
Tears, slow and caustic,
Pour out all by themselves.

But to him who quietly cries,
Standing silent by the window,
It already means nothing
That the problem is solved.

Только тёмная роза качнётся,
Лепестки осыпая на грудь.
Только сонная вечность проснётся
Для того, чтобы снова уснуть.

Паруса уплывают на север,
Поезда улетают на юг,
Через звёзды и пальмы, и клевер,
Через горе и счастье, мой друг.

Всё равно—не протягивай руки,
Всё равно—ничего не спасти.
Только синие волны разлуки,
Только синее слово «прости».

И рассеется дым паровоза,
И плеснёт, исчезая, весло . . .
Только вечность, как тёмная роза,
В мировое осыплется зло.

Only the dark rose will sway,
Scattering petals on the breast.
Only sleepy eternity will awaken
To fall asleep once more.

Sails sail off to the north,
Trains fly away to the south,
Through stars, and palms, and clover,
Through grief and happiness, my friend.

It's all the same—don't stretch out your arms,
It's all the same—nothing can be saved.
Only the blue waves of separation,
Only the blue word "forgive."

And the smoke of the locomotive dissipates,
And the oar splashes as it disappears . . .
Only eternity, like a dark rose,
Scatters into universal evil.

Я тебя не вспоминаю,
Для чего мне вспоминать?
Это только то, что знаю,
Только то, что можно знать.

Край земли. Полоска дыма
Тянет в небо, не спеша.
Одинока, нелюдима
Вьётся ласточкой душа.

Край земли. За синим краем
Вечности пустая гладь.
То, чего мы не узнаем,
То, чего не надо знать.

Если я скажу, что знаю,
Ты поверишь. Я солгу.
Я тебя не вспоминаю,
Не хочу и не могу.

Но люблю тебя, как прежде,
Может быть, ещё нежней,
Бессердечней, безнадёжней
В пустоте, в тумане дней.

I don't care to remember you,
Why should I bother?
This is the only thing I know,
The only thing that can be known.

The edge of the world. A band of smoke
Is drawn to the sky, leisurely.
Lonely, withdrawn
The soul soars like a swallow.

The edge of the world. Beyond the blue edge
Eternity's empty smooth expanse.
The thing we won't know,
The thing we need not know.

If I say I know,
You'll believe me. That would be a lie.
I don't care to remember you,
Don't want to and I can't.

But I love you like before,
Perhaps even more tenderly,
Heartlessly, hopelessly
In the emptiness, in the fog of days.

Над розовым морем вставала луна.
Во льду зеленела бутылка вина.

И томно кружились влюблённые пары
Под жалобный рокот гавайской гитары.

—Послушай. О, как это было давно,
Такое же море и то же вино.

Мне кажется, будто и музыка та же.
Послушай, послушай,—мне кажется даже . . .

—Нет, вы ошибаетесь, друг дорогой.
Мы жили тогда на планете другой.

И слишком устали, и слишком мы стары
Для этого вальса и этой гитары.

The moon came up over the rosy sea,
A bottle of wine shone green in the ice,

And enamored couples languidly circled
To the plaintive strumming of the ukulele.

Listen! O, how long ago it was
The very same sea, the very same wine.

It seems to me, it was the same music
Listen, listen—it even seems to me that . . .

—No, you are mistaken, dear friend.
Back then we lived on a different planet.

We're too tired, and too old
For this waltz and this guitar.

Это звон бубенцов издалёка,
Это тройки широкий разбег,
Это чёрная музыка Блока
На сияющий падает снег.

. . . За пределами жизни и мира,
В пропастях ледяного эфира
Всё равно не расстанусь с тобой!

И Россия, как белая лира,
Над засыпанной снегом судьбой.

It's the sound of yoke-bells from afar,
It's the wide running of a troika,
It's Blok's dark music
Falling on dazzling snow.

Beyond the bounds of life and the world,
In the abysses of the icy ether
No matter what, I'll not part with you!

And Russia, like a white lyre, hovers
Over our fate, buried in the snow.

В шуме ветра, в детском плаче,
В тишине, в словах прощанья
«А могло бы быть иначе»
Слышу я, как обещанье.

Одевает в саван нежный
Всю тщету, все неудачи —
Тень надежды безнадежной
«А могло бы быть иначе».

Заметает сумрак снежный
Все поля, все расстоянья.
Тень надежды безнадежной
Превращается в сиянье.

Все сгоревшие поленья,
Все решённые задачи,
Все слова, все преступленья . . .

А могло бы быть иначе.

In the sound of the wind, in a child's cry,
In silence, and in words of farewell
I hear, like a promise:
"It could have been different."

The shadow of hopeless hope
All the vanity, all the failures
Dressed in a tender shroud:
"It could have been different."

The snowy twilight sweeps
All fields, and all distances.
The shadow of hopeless hope
Transforms into a radiance.

All the burned logs,
All the solved problems,
All the words, all the crimes . . .

It could have been different.

Душа человека. Такою
Она не была никогда.
На небо глядела с тоскою,
Взволнованна, зла и горда.

И вот умирает. Так ясно,
Так просто сгорая дотла —
Легка, совершенна, прекрасна,
Нетленна, блаженна, светла.

Сиянье. Душа человека,
Как лебедь, поёт и грустит.
И крылья раскинув широко,
Над бурями тёмного века
В беззвёздное небо летит.

Над бурями тёмного рока
В сиянье. Всего не успеть . . .
Дым тянется . . . След остаётся . . .

И полною грудью поётся,
Когда уже не о чем петь.

The soul of a man. Never
Like this before.
Looking with longing to the sky,
Thrilled, evil, and proud.

And now it is dying. So clearly,
So simply, burning to a cinder—
Light, perfect, resplendent,
Everlasting, blissful, bright.

A radiance. The soul of a man,
Like a swan, it sings in sadness.
And throwing its wings out wide,
Flies above the storms of this dark age
Into the starless sky.

Above the storms of dark fate
Into the radiance. No time for everything . . .
The smoke spreads thin . . . A trace remains . . .

And you're singing your soul out,
When there is nothing to sing about.

Жизнь бессмысленную прожил
На ветру и на юру.
На минуту — будто ожил.
Что там. Полезай в дыру.

Он, не споря, покорился
И теперь в земле на век.
Так ничем не озарился
Скудный труд и краткий век.
Но . . . тоскует человек.

И ему в земле не спится
Или снится скверный сон . . .

В доме скрипнет половица,
На окошко сядет птица,
В стенке хрустнет. Это — он.

И тому, кто в доме, жутко
И ему — ох! — тяжело.
А была одна минутка.
Мог поймать. Не повезло.

He lived a senseless life
Tossed by the wind, chilled by a draft.
He seemed to come alive for a moment.
No use. Be quick, down into the hole.

Not resisting, he obeyed
And now he's in the ground forever.
All in all, nothing illuminated
His meager toil and his brief life.
Yet . . . He pines for something.

And he doesn't sleep well in the ground,
Or he dreams a bad dream . . .

At home a floorboard creaks,
A bird alights on a window,
Crackling in the wall. That's him.

And those in the house are horrified
And for him—my, how hard it is.
Yet there was a moment.
He could have captured it. No such luck.

ПОРТРЕТ БЕЗ СХОДСТВА
A PORTRAIT WITHOUT LIKENESS

(1950)

Посвящаю эту книгу Ирине Одоевцевой. —Г. И.

I dedicate this book to Irina Odoevtseva. —G. I.

Что-то сбудется, что-то не сбудется.
Перемелется всё, позабудется . . .

Но останется эта вот, рыжая,
У заборной калитки трава.

. . . Если плещется где-то Нева,
Если к ней долетают слова—
Это вам говорю из Парижа я
То, что сам понимаю едва.

Something will come true, something not;
Everything will be crushed, forgotten.

But this will remain, this rusty
Patch of grass by the fence gate.

If somewhere the Neva is splashing,
If these words fly there—
This is what I'm telling you from Paris,
Things I hardly understand myself.

Всё неизменно, и всё изменилось
В утреннем холоде странной свободы.
Долгие годы мне многое снилось,
Вот я проснулся—и где эти годы!

Вот я иду по осеннему полю,
Всё, как всегда, и другое, чем прежде:
Точно меня отпустили на волю
И отказали в последней надежде.

All is immutable, yet all has changed
In the morning chill of this strange freedom.
For long years I dreamed of many things,
Now I've awoken—and where are those years!

Now I walk along an autumn field,
All is the same, yet different than before:
Just as if I've been set free
And my last hope refused.

Друг друга отражают зеркала,
Взаимно искажая отраженья.

Я верю не в непобедимость зла,
А только в неизбежность пораженья.

Не в музыку, что жизнь мою сожгла,
А в пепел, что остался от сожженья.

Mirrors reflect each other,
Mutually distorting their reflections.

I believe not in the invincibility of evil,
But only in the unavoidability of defeat.

Not in the music that burned my life,
But in the ash left from the burning.

Маятника мерное качанье,
Полночь, одиночество, молчанье.

Старые счета перебираю.
Умереть? Да вот не умираю.

Тихо перелистываю «Розы» —
«Кабы на цветы да не морозы»!

The measured swing of the pendulum,
Midnight, loneliness, silence.

I sort through old reckonings.
Why don't I die? Well, so far I haven't.

I quietly leaf through *Roses*—
"If only the frost spared the flowers"!

Где прошлогодний снег, скажите мне?..
Нетаявший, почти альпийский снег,
Невинной жертвой отданный весне,
Апрелем обращённый в плеск и бег,
В дыханье одуванчиков и роз,
Взволнованного мира светлый вал,
В поэзию . . .
            В бессмысленный вопрос,
Что ей Виллон когда-то задавал.

Where are the snows of yesteryear, tell me?
Unmelting, almost Alpine snow,
An innocent victim given to spring,
Turned into splash and run by April,
Into the breath of dandelions and roses,
Into the bright billow of an anxious world,
Turned into poetry . . .

      Into the senseless question
Villon put to it once upon a time.

Воскресают мертвецы,
Наши деды и отцы,
Пращуры и предки.

Рвутся к жизни, как птенцы,
Из постылой клетки.

Вымирают города,
Мужики и господа,
Старички и детки.

И глядит на мир звезда,
Сквозь сухие ветки.

The dead are resurrected,
Our grandfathers and fathers,
Our forefathers and ancestors.

They rush to life, like fledglings
Exit their hated cage.

Cities die out,
Peasants and masters,
Little old men and kids.

And a star gazes at the world
Through dry branches.

Мёртвый проснётся в могиле,
Чёрная давит доска.
Что это? Что это?—Или
И воскресенье тоска?

И воскресенье унынье!
Скучное дело—домой . . .
Тянет Волынью, полынью,
Тянет сумой и тюрьмой.

И над соломой избёнок,
Сквозь косогоры и лес,
Жалобно плачет ребёнок,
Тот, что сегодня воскрес.

A corpse will awaken in his grave,
The dark coffin lid presses down.
What's this? What's this? Can
Resurrection be boredom, too?

Resurrection is despondency, too!
A tedious business—coming home . . .
Smells like Volhynia, wormwood,
Smells like a beggar's lot and jail.

And above thatched roofs,
Across slopes and forests,
A child plaintively cries,
The very one who today has risen.

Он спал, и Офелия снилась ему
В болотных огнях, в подвенечном дыму.

Она музыкальной спиралью плыла,
Как сон, отражали её зеркала.

Как нимб, окружали её светляки,
Как лес, вырастали за ней васильки . . .

. . . Как просто страдать. Можно душу отдать
И всё-таки сна не уметь передать.
И зная, что гибель стоит за плечом,
Грустить ни о ком, мечтать ни о чём . . .

He slept, and dreamed of Ophelia
In swamp fires, wrapped in wedding mist.

She swam in a musical spiral,
Mirrors reflected her, like a dream.

Like a nimbus, fireflies surrounded her,
Like a forest, cornflowers grew in her wake.

Suffering is so easy. You can give away your soul
And still not know how to express a dream.
And knowing death is at your shoulder,
Pine for no one, dream of nothing . . .

День превратился в своё отраженье,
В изнеможенье, головокруженье.

В звёзды и музыку день превратился.
Может быть, мир навсегда прекратился?

Что-то похожее было со мною,
Тоже у озера, тоже весною,

В синих и розовых сумерках тоже . . .
. . . Странно, что был я когда-то моложе.

The day has turned into its reflection,
Into exhaustion, dizziness.

The day has become stars and music.
Perhaps the world has ceased forever?

Something like that happened to me,
Also by a lake, also in spring,

Also in dark-blue and rose twilight . . .
Strange that once I was younger.

Рассказать обо всех мировых дураках,
Что судьбу человечества держат в руках?

Рассказать обо всех мертвецах-подлецах,
Что уходят в историю в светлых венцах?

Для чего?
            Тишина под парижским мостом.
И какое мне дело, что будет потом.

Should I tell of all the world-famous fools,
Who hold humanity's fate in their hands?

Should I tell of all the dead bastards,
Who enter history in shining wreaths?

What for?
       It's quiet under a Parisian bridge—
And why give a damn what comes next.

А люди? Ну на что мне люди?
Идёт мужик, ведёт быка.
Сидит торговка: ноги, груди,
Платочек, круглые бока.

Природа? Вот она, природа—
То дождь и холод, то жара.
Тоска в любое время года,
Как дребезжанье комара.

Конечно, есть и развлеченья:
Страх бедности, любви мученья,
Искусства сладкий леденец,
Самоубийство, наконец.

And people? So why do I need people?
Here's a peasant leading an ox.
Here sits a market woman: legs, breasts,
Cutesy kerchief, rounded flanks.

Nature? Well, here's nature—
Now it rains, now it's cold, then it's hot.
Dreariness at any season,
Like a mosquito's trembling buzz.

Sure, there are amusements:
The fear of poverty, love's torments,
The sweet lollipop of art,
And finally, there's suicide.

Образ полусотворённый,
Шопот недоговорённый,
Полужизнь, полуусталость —
Это всё, что мне осталось.

Принимаю, как награду,
Тень скользящую по саду,
Переход апреля к маю,
Как подарок, принимаю.

«Тот блажен кто забывает» —
Мудрость хоть и небольшая!..
...И забвенье наплывает,
Биться сердцу не мешая.

An image half-created,
A whisper not completed,
Half a life, half-weariness—
This is all that's left to me.

I accept as a reward
The shadow sliding through the garden,
The shift of April to May,
As a present, I accept it.

"He who forgets is blessed"
Wisdom it is, though not so great!
. . . And oblivion flows over me,
Not interfering with my beating heart.

В награду за мои грехи,
Позор и торжество,
Вдруг появляются стихи—
Вот так . . . Из ничего.

Всё кое-как и как-нибудь,
Волшебно на авось:
Как розы падают на грудь . . .

—И ты мне розу брось!

Нет, лучше брось за облака—
Там рифма заблестит,
Коснётся тленного цветка
И в вечный превратит.

As reward for my sins,
Shame and triumph,
There suddenly appear poems—
Just like that . . . Out of nothing.

Everything's askew and awry,
Magically, on the off chance:
Like roses fall upon your breast . . .

—You too, throw me a rose!

No, better throw it beyond the clouds—
There a rhyme will start to sparkle,
It'll touch the mortal flower
And turn it into an eternal one.

1

Я не стал ни лучше и ни хуже.
Под ногами тот же прах земной,
Только расстоянье стало уже
Между вечной музыкой и мной.

Жду, когда исчезнет расстоянье,
Жду, когда исчезнут все слова
И душа провалится в сиянье
Катастрофы или торжества.

1

I've become no better and no worse.
The same earthly dust under my feet,
Only the distance has become narrower
Between eternal music and me.

I wait for distance to vanish,
I wait for words to vanish
And for my soul to fall into a radiance
Of catastrophe or triumph.

2

Что ж, поэтом долго ли родиться . . .
Вот сумей поэтом умереть!
Собственным позором насладиться,
В собственной бессмыслице сгореть!

Разрушая, снова начиная,
Все автоматически губя,
В доказательство, что жизнь иная
Так же безнадежна, как земная,
Так же недоступна для тебя.

2

No, it doesn't take much to be born a poet:
But just you try dying as one!
Taking pleasure in your own disgrace,
Burning up in your own senselessness!

Tearing down, beginning again,
Automatically destroying all,
In proving that that other life is
Just as hopeless, as this earthly one,
Just as unattainable for you.

Холодно. В сумерках этой страны
Гибнут друзья, торжествуют враги.
Снятся мне в небе пустом
Белые звёзды над чёрным крестом.
　　И не слышны голоса и шаги,
　　Или почти не слышны.

Синие сумерки этой страны . . .
Всюду, куда ни посмотришь, — снега.
Жизнь положив на весы,
Вижу, что жизнь мне не так дорога.
　　И не страшны мне ночные часы,
　　Или почти не страшны . . .

Cold. In the twilight of this country
Friends perish, enemies triumph.
In a dream I see in an empty sky
White stars over a black cross.
 And voices and steps are not audible,
 Or almost not audible.

The deep-blue twilights of this country . . .
Wherever you look—snow everywhere.
Having put life on the scales,
I see that life is not so precious to me.
 And the night hours are not terrifying,
 Or almost not terrifying . . .

Тихим вечером в тихом саду
Облака отражались в пруду.

Ангел нёс в бесконечность звезду
И её уронил над прудом . . .

И стоит заколоченный дом,
И молчит заболоченный пруд,
Скоро в нём и лягушки умрут.

И лежишь на болотистом дне,
Ты, сиявшая мне в вышине.

One quiet evening in a quiet garden
Clouds were reflected in the pond.

An angel carried a star into infinity
And let it drop over the pond . . .

And there stands a boarded-up house,
And the stagnant pond is silent,
Soon even the frogs in it will die.

And you lie at the swampy bottom,
You, who shone to me from on high.

Каждой ночью грозы
Не дают мне спать.
Отцветают розы
И цветут опять.
Точно в мир спустилась
Вечная весна,
Точно распустилась
Розами война.

Тишины всемирной
Голубая тьма.
Никогда так мирны
Не были дома
И такою древней
Не была земля . . .
. . . Тишина деревни,
Тополя, поля.

Вслушиваясь в слабый,
Нежный шум ветвей
Поджидают бабы
Мёртвых сыновей:

В старости опора
Каждому нужна,
А теперь уж скоро
Кончится война!

The storms won't let me
Sleep at night.
Roses fade
And bloom again.
As if eternal spring
Descended into the world,
Just as if the war
Opened wide like roses.

The sky-blue darkness
Of universal silence.
The houses have
Never been so peaceful
And the earth has
Never been so ancient.
The silence of the village,
Poplars, fields.

Listening carefully to the weak
Tender noise of the branches
Peasant women await
Their dead sons:

Everyone needs
Support in old age,
And now already,
Soon the war will end!

Был замысел странно-порочен
И всё-таки жизнь подняла
В тумане — туманные очи
И два лебединых крыла.

И всё-таки тени качнулись
Пока догорала свеча.
И всё-таки струны рванулись,
Бессмысленным счастьем звуча . . .

The design was strangely flawed
But all the same, in the mist, life
Raised its misty eyes
And two swan wings.

But all the same, the shadows swayed
While the candle was burning.
But all the same, the strings strained,
With the sound of senseless happiness . . .

Потеряв даже в прошлое веру,
Став ни это, мой друг, и ни то, —
Уплываем теперь на Цитеру
В синеватом сияньи Ватто . . .

Грусть любуется лунным пейзажем,
Смерть, как парус, шумит за кормой . . .
. . . Никому ни о чём не расскажем,
Никогда не вернёмся домой.

Losing even faith in the past,
Becoming, my friend, neither this nor that—
We sail now for Cythera
In the deep blue radiance of Watteau . . .

Sadness admires a moonlit scene,
Death like a sail sounds off the stern . . .
We won't tell anything to anyone,
We will never return home.

Отражая волны голубого света,
В направленьи Ниццы пробежал трамвай.
Задавай вопросы. Не проси ответа.
Лучше и вопросов, друг, не задавай.

Улыбайся морю. Наслаждайся югом.
Помни, что в России — ночь и холода,
Помни, что тебя я называю другом,
Зная, что не встречу нигде и никогда . . .

Reflecting the waves of the sky-blue light,
A tram hurried by, heading for Nice.
Ask questions. Don't request an answer.
Better still, my friend, don't ask any questions.

Smile at the sea. Enjoy the South.
Remember, in Russia—it's dark and cold,
Remember, I call you my friend,
Knowing I'll meet you nowhere and never.

Ничего не вернуть. И зачем возвращать?
Разучились любить, разучились прощать,
Забывать никогда не научимся . . .

Спит спокойно и сладко чужая страна.
Море ровно шумит. Наступает весна
В этом мире в котором мы мучимся.

You can return nothing. And why bother?
We've unlearned how to love, how to forgive.
How to forget, we will never learn . . .

This alien land's sleep is calm and sweet.
The sea heaves evenly. Spring enters
Into the world of our torment.

На грани таянья и льда
Зеленоватая звезда.

На грани музыки и сна
Полу-зима, полу-весна,

К невесте тянется жених,
И звёзды падают на них,

Летят сквозь снежную фату,
В сияющую пустоту.

Ты—это я. Я—это ты.
Слова нежны. Сердца пусты.

Я—это ты. Ты—это я
На хрупком льду небытия.

On the border of melt and ice
There is a greenish star.

On the border of music and dream
Half-winter, half-spring,

The groom reaches out to his bride,
And stars fall upon them,

They fly through the snowy bridal veil
Into a radiant emptiness.

You are I. I am you.
Tender words, empty hearts.

I am you. You are I
On the fragile ice of nonexistence.

Отвратительнейший шум на свете —
Грохот авиона на рассвете . . .

И зачем тебя, наш дом, разбили?
Ты был маленький, волшебный дом,
Как ребёнка, мы тебя любили,
Строили тебя с таким трудом.

The most revolting noise in the world—
The roar of an aeroplane at daybreak . . .

And why did they have to smash you, our dear house?
You were a small, charming house,
We loved you like a child,
We built you with so much effort.

Как туман на рассвете — чужая душа.
И прохожий в неё заглянул не спеша,
Улыбнулся и дальше пошёл . . .

Было утро какого-то летнего дня.
Солнце встало, шиповник расцвёл
Для людей, для тебя, для меня . . .

Можно вспомнить о Боге и Бога забыть,
Можно душу свою навсегда погубить
Или душу навеки спасти —

Оттого, что шиповнику время цвести
И цветущая ветка качнулась в саду,
Где сейчас я с тобою иду.

The soul of another is like a mist at dawn . . .
A passerby looked in at it unhurriedly,
Smiled and walked on . . .

It was the morning of some summer day.
The sun had risen, the eglantine was in bloom
For people, for you, for me . . .

One may return to God, or forget Him,
One can bury one's soul for good
Or save one's soul forever—

Because it is the time for the eglantine to bloom
And a blooming branch swayed in the garden,
Where you and I are walking now.

Поговори со мной о пустяках,
О вечности поговори со мной.
Пусть, как ребёнок, на твоих руках
Лежат цветы, рождённые весной.

Так беззаботна ты и так грустна.
Как музыка, ты можешь всё простить.
Ты так же беззаботна, как весна,
И, как весна, не можешь не грустить.

Speak to me of trifles,
Of eternity speak to me.
Let flowers born in spring
Lie like a babe in your arms.

You are so carefree and so sad.
Like music, you may forgive everything.
You are as carefree as spring,
And, like spring, you cannot but be sad.

Лунатик в пустоту глядит,
Сиянье им руководит,
Чернеет гибель снизу.
И даже угадать нельзя,
Куда он движется, скользя,
По лунному карнизу.

Расстреливают палачи
Невинных в мировой ночи—
Не обращай вниманья!
Гляди в холодное ничто,
В сияньи постигая то,
Что выше пониманья.

A sleepwalker looks into emptiness,
A radiance is guiding him;
Death gapes black from below.
And one cannot even guess
Where he is headed, sliding
Along the lunar ledge.

Executioners shoot
The innocent in the world's night—
Don't pay any attention!
Look into the cold nothingness,
Comprehending in the radiance,
What is beyond understanding.

Летний вечер прозрачный и грузный.
Встала радуга коркой арбузной.
Вьётся птица—крылатый булыжник . . .
Так на небо глядел передвижник,
Оптимист и искусства подвижник.

Он был прав. Мы с тобою не правы.
Берегись декадентской отравы:
«Райских звёзд», искажённого света,
Упоенья сомнительной славы,
Неизбежной расплаты за это.

This summer evening is transparent and bloated.
A rainbow rises like a watermelon rind.
A bird soars—a stone with wings . . .
Thus an Itinerant looked at the sky,
An optimist and promoter of the arts.

He was right. You and I are wrong.
Beware of Decadent poison:
"Stars of Paradise," the distorted light,
The thrill of dubious glory,
The inevitable reckoning for all that.

Шаг направо. Два налево.
И опять стена.
Смотрит сквозь окошко хлева
Белая луна.

Шаг налево. Два направо.
На соломе — кровь . . .
Где они, надменность, слава,
Молодость, любовь? . .

Всё слила пустого хлева
Грязная стена.
Улыбнитесь, королева,
Вечность — вот она!

Впереди палач и плаха,
Верность вся, в упор!
Улыбнитесь. И с размаха —
Упадёт топор.

A step to the right. Two to the left.
And again a wall.
The white moon
Stares through the pigsty window.

A step to the left. Two to the right.
Blood on the straw.
Where are they: arrogance, glory,
Youth, love?

Everything fused together the filthy wall
Of this empty pigsty.
Smile, my queen,
Eternity—here it is!

Ahead—the executioner and the scaffold,
All the loyalty, right at you!
Smile. And in one fell swoop
The ax will drop.

Теперь тебя не уничтожат,
Как тот безумный вождь мечтал.
Судьба поможет, Бог поможет,
Но—русский человек устал . . .

Устал страдать, устал гордиться,
Валя куда-то напролом.
Пора забвеньем насладиться
А, может быть—пора на слом . . .

. . . И ничему не возродиться
Ни под серпом, ни под орлом!

They won't destroy you now,
The way that insane leader dreamed.
Fate will help, God will help,
But the Russian man has grown tired . . .

Tired of suffering, tired of being proud,
Rushing somewhere, breaking through.
Time to enjoy oblivion
But perhaps it's time to be scrapped.

There's to be no reviving,
Not by the Sickle, nor by the Eagle.

Стоило ли этого счастье безрассудное?
Всё-таки возможное? О, конечно, да.
Птицей улетевшее в небо изумрудное,
Где переливается вечерняя звезда.

Будьте легкомысленней! Будьте легковернее!
Если вам не спится — выдумывайте сны.
Будьте, если можете, как звезда вечерняя,
Так же упоительны, так же холодны.

This reckless yet attainable joy,
Was it worth it after all? O, surely, yes.
Like a bird flown off into an emerald sky,
Where the Evening Star glimmers.

Be more thoughtless, more gullible!
If sleep does not come—dream up dreams.
Be, if you can, like the Evening Star,
Just as ravishing, just as cold.

Ветер тише, дождик глуше,
И на всё один ответ:

Корабли увидят сушу,
Мёртвые увидят свет.

Ежедневной жизни муку
Я и так едва терплю.
За ритмическую скуку,
Дождик, я тебя люблю.

Барабанит, барабанит,
Барабанит, — ну и пусть,
А когда совсем устанет
И моя устанет грусть.

В самом деле — что я трушу:
Хуже страха вещи нет.
Ну и потеряю душу,
Ну и не увижу свет.

The wind dies down, the light rain softens,
And there is but one answer:

Ships will see dry land,
The dead will see the light.

As it is I can barely tolerate
Life's everyday torture.
Light rain, I love you
For your rhythmic boredom.

You drum, drum,
Drum—well so be it.
And when it all comes to a stop
Then too will my sadness cease.

And really—why be a coward—
There's nothing worse than fear.
So what, I'll lose my soul,
So what, I won't see the light.

По дому бродит полуночник —
То улыбнётся, то вздохнёт,
То ослабевший позвоночник
Над письменным столом согнёт.

Черкнёт и бросит. Выпьет чаю,
Загрезит чем-то наяву.
. . . Нельзя сказать, что я скучаю.
Нельзя сказать, что я живу.

Не обижаясь, не жалея,
Не вспоминая, не грустя . . .

. . . Так труп в песке лежит не тлея,
И так рожденья ждёт дитя.

The night owl wanders about the house—
Now he smiles, now he sighs,
Now he bends his weakened spine
Over his writing desk.

He scribbles, he stops. Drinks some tea,
Then falls into daydreaming.
You can't say I'm bored,
You can't say that I'm alive.

No taking offense, no regretting,
No remembering, no sadness . . .

Thus a corpse lies in the sand, not rotting,
Thus a child awaits its birth.

С бесчеловечною судьбой
Какой же спор? Какой же бой?
Всё это наважденье.

. . . Но этот вечер голубой
Ещё мое владенье.

И небо. Красно меж ветвей,
А по краям жемчужно . . .
Свистит в сирени соловей,
Ползёт по травке муравей—
Кому-то это нужно.

Пожалуй, нужно даже то,
Что я вдыхаю воздух,
Что старое моё пальто
Закатом слева залито,
А справа тонет в звёздах.

With this inhuman fate
Is there any arguing? Any fighting?
It's all delusion.

Yet this pale-blue night
Is still my dominion.

And the sky—red among the branches,
Pearl-hued along the edges . . .
A nightingale whistles in a lilac bush,
An ant crawls along a blade of grass—
Someone needs those things.

Perhaps, my breathing in the air,
Even that is needed,
That my old overcoat
Is flooded on the left by the sunset,
And on the right drowns in the stars.

Если бы жить . . . Только бы жить . . .
Хоть на литейном заводе служить.

Хоть углекопом с тяжелой киркой,
Хоть бурлаком над Великой Рекой.

«Ухнем, дубинушка . . .»
            Всё это сны.
Руки твои ни на что не нужны.

Этим плечам ничего не поднять.
Нечего, значит, на Бога пенять.

Трубочка есть. Водочка есть,
Всем в кабаке одинакова честь!

If I could live, only live,
Even to work in a foundry.

Even to be a coal miner with a heavy pickax.
Even to be a barge hauler on the Great River.

"Let's pull now, heave . . ."
         That's just dreams.
Your arms are good for nothing.

These shoulders won't lift a thing—
There is nothing to blame God for.

Got your pipe, got your shot of vodka,
In this watering hole everyone's treated the same.

В дыму, в огне, в сияньи, в кружевах,
И веерах, и страусовых перьях!..
В сухих цветах, в бессмысленных словах,
И в грешных снах и в детских суеверьях —

Так женщина смеётся на балу,
Так беззаконная звезда летит во мглу...

Amid smoke, fire, radiance, and lace,
Amid fans and ostrich feathers!
Amid dried flowers, senseless words,
In sinful dreams and childish superstitions—

That is how a woman laughs at a ball,
That is how a lawless star flies into the dark.

Восточные поэты пели
Хвалу цветам и именам,
Догадываясь еле-еле
О том, что недоступно нам.

Но эта смутная догадка
Полу-мечта, полу-хвала.
Вся разукрашенная сладко,
Тем ядовитее была.

Сияла ночь Омар-Хаяму,
Свистел персидский соловей,
И розы заплетали яму,
Могильных полную червей.

Быть может, высшая надменность:
То развлекаться, то скучать.
Сквозь пальцы видеть современность,
О самом главном — промолчать.

The Oriental poets sang
Praises to names and flowers,
Hardly, hardly guessing at
Things unattainable to us.

But that troubling guess
Half-dream, half-praise,
All sweetly decked out,
Was all the more poisonous.

The night blazed for Omar Khayyám,
The Persian nightingale whistled,
And roses overgrew a pit
Teeming with sepulchral worms.

Perhaps it is the height of arrogance:
Now you enjoy yourself, now you're bored.
Not paying much attention to modernity,
Remaining silent about the main thing.

Остановиться на мгновенье,
Взглянуть на Сену и дома,
Испытывая вдохновенье,
Почти сводящее с ума.

Оно никак не воплотится,
Но через годы и века
Такой же луч зазолотится
Сквозь гаснущие облака,

Сливая счастье и страданье
В неясной прелести земной . . .
И это будет оправданье
Всего, погубленного мной.

To stop for a moment,
To look at the Seine and the houses,
Experiencing inspiration,
Which almost drives you mad.

It will in no way become reality,
Yet over the years and centuries
The same kind of ray will shine golden
Through the fading clouds,

Merging happiness and suffering
In the world's vague charm . . .
And this will be justification
Of all that has been ruined by me.

У входа в бойни, сквозь стальной туман,
Поскрипывая, полз подъёмный кран,
И ледяная чешуя канала
Венецию слегка напоминала . . .

А небо было в розах и в огне
Таких, что сердце начинало биться . . .
Как будто всё обещанное мне
Сейчас, немедленно, осуществится.

Scraping, the crane crawled through
The steely fog, past the entryway of the slaughterhouse,
And the icy scales of the canal
Reminded me a bit of Venice . . .

And the sky was in roses and fire
Such that my heart would begin to beat,
As if all that had been promised to me
Must now, immediately, come true.

То, о чём искусство лжёт,
Ничего не открывая,
То, что сердце бережёт—
Вечный свет, вода живая . . .

Остальное пустяки.
Вьются у зажжённой свечки
Комары и мотыльки,
Суетятся человечки,
Умники и дураки.

That about which art tells lies,
Discovering nothing;
That which the heart treasures—
Eternal light, living water . . .

The rest is trifles.
Mosquitoes and moths
Swirl about a lit candle,
Homunculi crowd about,
Brainy ones and idiots.

В конце концов судьба любая
Могла бы быть моей судьбой.
От безразличья погибая,
Гляжу на вечер голубой:

Домишки покосились вправо
Под нежным натиском веков,
А дальше тишина и слава
Весны, заката, облаков.

After all, anyone's fate
Could have been mine.
Dying of indifference
I stare at the pale-blue evening:

Huts have leaned to the right
Under the tender pressure of the centuries,
Further on lies the quiet and the glory
Of spring, of sunset, of the clouds.

Rayon de rayonne

1

В тишине вздохнула жаба.
Из калитки вышла баба
В ситцевом платке.

Сердце бьется слабо, слабо,
Будто вдалеке.

В светлом небе пусто, пусто.
Как ядрёная капуста
Катится луна.

И бессмыслица искусства
Вся, насквозь, видна . . .

Rayon de rayonne

1

In the quiet a toad sighed.
A peasant woman came out from her gate
Wearing a calico kerchief.

The heart beats weakly, weakly,
As if from afar.

The bright sky empty, empty.
The moon rolls by
Like a hearty cabbage.

And the ridiculousness of Art
Becomes visible, through and through.

Портной обновочку утюжит,
Сопит портной, шипит утюг,
И брюки выглядит не хуже
Любых обыкновенных брюк.

А между тем они из воска,
Из музыки, из лебеды,
На синем белая полоска—
Граница счастья и беды.

Из бездны протянулись руки:
В одной цветы, в другой кинжал . . .
Вскочил портной, спасая брюки,
Но никуда не убежал.

Торчит кинжал в боку портного.
Белеют розы на груди.
В сияньи брюки Ивано́ва
Летят и—вечность впереди.

The tailor irons a new order,
The tailor sniffles, the iron sizzles,
And the pants look no worse
Than any other ordinary pants.

But at the same time they're made of wax,
Of music, of goosefoot leaves,
Across the dark blue runs a white stripe—
The border of happiness and woe.

Two hands stretch out from the abyss:
In one, flowers, in the other a dagger . . .
The tailor leaps up, saving the pants,
But there was nowhere to escape for him.

The dagger sticks out of the tailor's side,
Roses shine white on his chest,
In this radiance the pants of Ivanóv
Are flying—and eternity lies ahead.

3

Всё чаще эти объявления:
Однополчане и семья
Вновь выражают сожаленья . . .
«Сегодня ты, а завтра я!»

Мы вымираем по порядку —
Кто поутру, кто вечерком.
И на кладбищенскую грядку
Ложимся, ровенько, рядком.

Невероятно до смешного:
Был целый мир — и нет его . . .

Вдруг — ни похода ледяного,
Ни капитана Ивано́ва,
Ну абсолютно ничего!

3

These announcements come more often:
Your comrades-in-arms and family
Once again offer their condolences . . .
"Today it's your turn, tomorrow mine!"

We're dying off one by one—
One in the morning, another at night
And we lie in a cemetery patch
Quite evenly, side by side.

It's incredible, almost a joke:
There was a whole world—and now it's gone . . .

Suddenly—no Ice March,
No Captain Ivanóv,
Absolutely nothing, nothing at all!

4

Где-то белые медведи
На таком же белом льду
Повторяют «буки-веди»,
Принимаясь за еду.

Где-то рыжие верблюды
На оранжевом песке
Опасаются простуды,
Напевая «бре-ке-ке».

Всё всегда, когда-то, где-то
Время глупое ползёт.
Мне шестериком карета
Ничего не привезёт.

4

Somewhere white bears
On this same white ice
Repeat by heart their ABCs,
Getting down to dinner.

Somewhere red-haired camels
On orange sands
Scare off the chill,
Singing "crow-crow-croak."

As always—sometime, somewhere—
Dumb time is crawling along.
A six-horse carriage
Won't be bringing anything to me.

А от цево? Никто не ведает притцыны.

Фонвизин

По улице уносит стружки
Ноябрский ветер ледяной.
— Вы русский? — Ну, понятно, рушкий.
Нос бесконечный. Шарф смешной.

Есть у него жена и дети,
Своя мечта, своя беда.
— Как скучно жить на этом свете,
Как неуютно, господа!

Обедать, спать, болеть поносом.
Немножко красть. — А кто не крал?
. . . Такой же Гоголь с длинным носом
Так долго, страшно умирал . . .

5

An' why? No one know the reeson.

                                                Fonvizin

An icy November wind
Carries scraps along the street.
"Are you Russian?" "Sure thing, Rooshin."
Endless nose, ridiculous scarf.

He's got a wife and children,
His own dreams, his own woes.
"How boring to live in this world,
How uncomfortable, ladies and gentlemen!"

To dine, to sleep, to suffer from diarrhea.
To steal a bit. "And who has not stolen, anyway?"
. . . Gogol, with the same long nose,
Lingered on too, dying a horrible death . . .

6

Зазеваешься, мечтая,
Дрогнет удочка в руке—
Вот и рыбка золотая
На серебряном крючке.

Так мгновенно, так прелестно—
Солнце, ветер и вода—
Даже рыбке в речке тесно,
Даже ей нужна беда.

Нужно, чтобы небо гасло,
Лодка ластилась к воде,
Чтобы закипало масло
Нежно на сковороде.

6

Daydreaming, you begin to drift off,
And the fishing pole trembles in your hand.
Well, here's a little golden fish
Caught on a silver hook.

So suddenly, so charmingly—
The sun, the wind and water—
Even the little fish feels crowded in the river,
Even it needs misfortune.

It is necessary that the sky grew dim,
That the rowboat snuggled to the water,
That the butter began to sizzle
Tenderly in the frying pan.

Снова море, снова пальмы
И гвоздики, и песок,
Снова вкрадчиво-печальный
Этой птички голосок.

Никогда её не видел
И не знаю, какова.
Кто её навек обидел,
В чём, своём, она права?

Велика или невеличка?
Любит воду иль лесок?
Может, и совсем не птичка,
А из ада голосок?

Once again the sea, once again the palms
And carnations, and sand,
Once again the insinuatingly sad,
Wee voice of that little bird.

I've never seen it,
I don't know its kind.
Who wronged it for all time,
In what way is it in its rights?

Is it big or is it tiny?
Does it like the water or the woods?
Perhaps it's not a bird at all,
But a little voice from hell?

8

Добровольно, до срока,
(Всё равно—решено),
Не окончив урока,
Опускайтесь на дно.

С неизбежным не споря,
(Волноваться смешно),
У лазурного моря
Допивайте вино!

Улыбнитесь друг другу
И снимайтесь с земли,
Треугольником, к югу,
Как вдали журавли . . .

8

Voluntary, ahead of time,
(It's been determined all the same),
Without finishing the lesson,
Sink to the bottom.

No arguing with the inevitable,
(It's ridiculous to be nervous),
Drink up your wine
By the azure sea!

Smile to each other,
Take off from the earth,
And in flight formation head south,
Like those distant cranes.

В пышном доме графа Зубова
О блаженстве, о Италии
Тенор пел. С румяных губ его
Звуки, тая, улетали и . . .

За окном, шумя полозьями,
Пешеходами, трамваями,
Гаснул, как в туманном озере,
Петербург незабываемый.

. . . Абажур зажёгся матово
В голубой, овальной комнате.
Нежно гладя пса лохматого,
Предсказала мне Ахматова:
«Этот вечер вы запомните».

9

In Count Zuboff's splendid house
A tenor sang of bliss, of Italy;
The sounds, melting, flew from
His rosy lips, and . . .

Outside the window, in the noise of sleighs,
Pedestrians and trams,
Petersburg the unforgettable,
Faded away, as in a misty lake.

In the sky-blue oval room
In the suffused light of a lamp shade,
Tenderly stroking a shaggy-haired dog,
Akhmatova prophesied to me:
"You will remember this night."

Имя тебе непонятное дали,
Ты — забытьё.
Или — точнее — цианистый калий
Имя твоё.

Георгий Адамович

Как вы когда-то разборчивы были,
О, дорогие мои!
Водки не пили — ее не любили —
Предпочитали Нюи . . .

Стал нашим хлебом цианистый калий,
Нашей водой — сулема.
Что ж — притерпелись и попривыкали,
Не посходили с ума.

Даже напротив — в бессмысленно-злобном
Мире — противимся злу:
Ласково кружимся в вальсе загробном,
На эмигрантском балу.

They have given you an
incomprehensible name,
You are oblivion.
Or—more precisely—cyanide
That is your name.

Georgy Adamovich

How fastidious were you once,
O, my dear friends!
No drinking vodka, you didn't like it,
You preferred the Nuits . . .

Cyanide became our bread,
Chloride, our water.
Even so, we endured, grew used to,
We didn't go mad.

Just the opposite—in this insane-spiteful
World—we resist evil:
Sweetly twirling in a deathly waltz,
At an émigré ball.

1943–1958

СТИХИ

POEMS

(1958)

ПОРТРЕТ БЕЗ СХОДСТВА

Игра судьбы. Игра добра и зла.
Игра ума. Игра воображенья.
«Друг друга отражают зеркала,
Взаимно искажая отраженья . . .»

Мне говорят — ты выиграл игру!
Но всё равно. Я больше не играю.
Допустим, как поэт я не умру,
Зато как человек я умираю.

To Irina Odoevtseva

A PORTRAIT WITHOUT LIKENESS

A game of fate. A game of good and evil.
A game of mind. A game of imagination.
"Mirrors reflect each other,
Mutually distorting their reflections . . ."

They tell me, "You've won the game!"
It's all the same. I'm not playing anymore.
All right, as a poet I will not die,
Yet as a man I am dying.

RAYON DE RAYONNE

Голубизна чужого моря,
Блаженный вздох весны чужой
Для нас скорей эмблема горя,
Чем символ прелести земной.

. . . Фитиль, любитель керосина,
Затрепетал, вздохнул, потух —
И внемлет арфе Серафима
В священном ужасе петух.

RAYON DE RAYONNE

The bright blue of an alien sea,
The blessed sigh of an alien spring
For us this is more like an emblem of woe
Than a symbol of earthly delight.

The wick, a kerosene lover,
Flickered, sighed, and went out—
And a rooster, awe-stricken
Gives ear to the harp of a Seraph.

Вот более иль менее
Приехали в имение.
Вот менее иль более
Дорожки, клумбы, поле и
Всё то, что пологается,
Чтоб дачникам утешиться:
Идёт старик—ругается,
Сидит собака—чешется.

И более иль менее—
На всём недоумение.

Well, more or less
We've arrived at the estate.
Well, less or more
Little lanes, flower beds, a field
And all the stuff that's needed
For bungalow folk to find comfort:
An old man comes along, cursing,
A dog sits, scratching itself.

And more or less,
It's all a mess.

Что мне нравится — того я не имею,
Что хотел бы делать — делать не умею.

Мне моё лицо, походка, даже сны
Головокружительно скучны.

—Как же так? Позволь . . . Да что с тобой такое?
—Ах, любезный друг, оставь меня в покое! . .

What I like—I don't possess,
What I'd like to do—I don't know how.

For me, my face, my gait, even
My dreams are dizzyingly boring.

"How so? Wait, what's wrong with you?"
"Oh, you know what, leave me alone!"

На полянке поутру
Веселился кенгуру —
Хвостик собственный кусал,
В воздух лапочки бросал.

Тут же рядом камбала
Водку пила, ром пила,
Раздевалась догола,
Напевала тра-ла-ла,
Любовалась в зеркала . . .

— Тра-ла-ла-ла-ла-ла-ла,
Я флакон одеколону
Не жалея, извела,
Вертебральную колонну
Оттирая добела!

In a clearing in the morning dew
Enjoyed himself a kangaroo—
Munch did he his own small tail,
Threw his paws into the air.

Right next to him a real live flounder
Swilling vodka, and rum straight down 'er,
Took off her clothes until quite naked
Crooning away with tra-la-la,
Admired herself in her mirror . . .

Tra-la-la-la-la-la-la,
Eau de Cologne I took a flask
And mercilessly applied some,
My vertebral column nearly smashed
I rubbed it white and then some!

Художников развязная мазня,
Поэтов выспренняя болтовня . . .

Гляжу на это рабское старанье,
Испытывая жалость и тоску:

Насколько лучше — блеянье баранье,
Мычанье, кваканье, кукуреку.

Artists' unbridled daubs,
Poets' highfalutin' babble . . .

I look at all that slavish striving,
Feeling pity and anguish:

How much better—bah-bah bleating,
Mooing, quacking, cock-a-doodle-dooing.

ДНЕВНИК

Торжественно кончается весна,
И розы, как в эдеме, расцвели.
Над океаном блеск и тишина,
И в блеске—паруса и корабли . . .

. . . Узнает ли когда-нибудь она,
Моя невероятная страна,
Что было солью каторжной земли?

А впрочем, соли всюду грош цена.
Просыпали—метелкой подмели.

DIARY

Spring triumphantly draws to a close
And roses are in bloom, as in Eden.
There is brightness and silence over the sea
And in that shimmer—sails and ships . . .

. . . Will she ever find out,
That improbable country of mine,
What was the salt of this imprisoned earth?

Still, salt goes for a song everywhere;
Strewn about—swept away.

Калитка закрылась со скрипом,
Осталась в пространстве заря,
И к благоухающим липам
Приблизился свет фонаря.

И влажно они просияли
Курчавою тенью сквозной,
Как отблеск на одеяле,
Свечей, сквозь дымок отходной.

И важно они прошумели,
Как будто посмели теперь
Сказать то, чего не умели,
Пока не захлопнулась дверь.

The gate closed with a creak,
Dawn lingered in space,
And the streetlight grew closer
To the fragrant linden trees.

And they shone forth moistly
Through their frayed, curly shade,
Like a reflection on a blanket,
Of candles, smoke, last rites.

And they sounded forth with importance,
As if now they dared
To say that which they could not,
Until the door slammed shut.

Эмалевый крестик в петлице
И серой тужурки сукно . . .
Какие печальные лица
И как это было давно.

Какие прекрасные лица
И как безнадежно бледны —
Наследник, императрица,
Четыре великих княжны . . .

Small enamel cross in his lapel,
Gray cloth of his blouse . . .
Such sad faces,
And how long ago it was.

Such wonderful faces
And how hopelessly pale—
Tsarevich, Empress,
Four Grand Duchesses . . .

Теперь, когда я сгнил и черви обглодали
До блеска остов мой и удалились прочь,
Со мной случилось то, чего не ожидали
Ни те, кто мне вредил, ни кто хотел помочь.

Любезные друзья, не стоил я презренья,
Прелестные враги, помочь вы не могли.
Мне исковеркал жизнь талант двойного зренья,
Но даже черви им, увы, пренебрегли.

Now that I've decayed and worms have picked me
To a shining skeleton and have gone away,
I've become what no one expected,
Neither those who wished me harm, or well.

Obliging friends, I wasn't worth your contempt;
Charming enemies, you couldn't help.
My life was wrecked by a talent for double vision,
But even the worms scorned it, alas.

Смилостивилась погода,
Дождик перестал.
Час от часу, год от года,
Как же я устал!

Даже не отдать отчёта,
Боже, до чего!
Ни надежды. Ни расчёта.
Просто — ничего.

Прожиты тысячелетья
В чёрной пустоте.
И не прочь бы умереть я,
Если бы не «те».

«Те» иль «эти»? «Те» иль «эти»?
Ах, не всё ль равно,
(Перед тем, как в лунном свете
Улететь в окно).

The weather had mercy,
The drizzle stopped.
Hour after hour, year after year
How tired I am!

Couldn't even account for,
My God, how much!
No hope, no forethought,
Simply nothing.

Millennia have passed
In black emptiness.
I wouldn't be averse to dying,
If it weren't for "those."

"Those" or "these"? "These" or "those"?
Ah, isn't it all the same,
(Before flying out the window
By the light of the moon).

«Желтофиоль» — похоже на виолу,
На меланхолию, на канифоль.
Иллюзия относится к Эолу,
Как к белизне — безмолвие и боль.
И, подчиняясь рифмы произволу,
Мне всё равно — пароль или король.

Поэзия — точнейшая наука:
Друг друга отражают зеркала,
Срывается с натянутого лука
Отравленная музыкой стрела
И в пустоту летит, быстрее звука . . .

« . . . Оставь меня. Мне ложе стелит скука»!

"Yellow violet"—sounds like "viola,"
Melancholy, rosin.
Illusion relates to Aeolus,
As whiteness to silence and pain.
And, submitting to the will of rhythm,
I care not if it is "ring" or "king."

Poetry, a most exacting science:
Mirrors reflect each other,
An arrow poisoned with music
Breaks forth from the taut bow and
Flies into emptiness, faster than sound . . .

"Leave me. Boredom makes my bed!"

Этой жизни нелепость и нежность
Проходя, как под тёплым дождём,
Знаем мы — впереди неизбежность,
Но её появленья не ждём.

И, проснувшись от резкого света,
Видим вдруг — неибежность пришла,
Как в безоблачном небе комета,
Лучезарная вестница зла.

Passing by the absurdity and tenderness
Of this life, as in a warm rain,
We know—ahead lies the inevitable,
Yet its arrival surprises all the same.

And, awakened by a sharp light,
We suddenly see: the inevitable has come,
Like a comet in a cloudless sky,
A radiant harbinger of evil.

Мелодия становится цветком,
Он распускается и осыпается,
Он делается ветром и песком,
Летящим на огонь весенним мотыльком,
Ветвями ивы в воду опускается . . .

Проходит тысяча мгновенных лет,
И перевоплощается мелодия
В тяжелый взгляд, в сиянье эполет,
В рейтузы, в ментик, в «Ваше благородие»,
В корнета гвардии — о, почему бы нет? . .

Туман . . . Тамань . . . Пустыня внемлет Богу.
— Как далеко до завтрашнего дня! . .

И Лермонтов один выходит на дорогу,
Серебряными шпорами звеня.

Melody becomes a flower,
It blossoms and scatters,
It turns into wind and sand,
Flying into the flame like a spring moth,
Like willow branches dipping into the water.

A thousand instantaneous years pass by,
And the melody transforms
Into an intense stare, gleaming epaulets,
Riding breeches, a pelisse, and "Your Honor,"
Into a cornet of the guards—and why not?

Mist . . . Taman . . . The desert gives heed to God.
How far it is until tomorrow!

And Lermontov alone comes out onto the road,
His silver spurs jingling.

Владимиру Маркову

Полутона рябины и малины
В Шотландии рассыпанные втуне,
В меланхоличном имени Алины,
В голубоватом золоте латуни.

Сияет жизнь улыбкой изумлённой,
Растит цветы, расстреливает пленных,
И входит гость в Коринф многоколонный,
Чтоб изнемочь в объятьях вожделенных!

В упряжке скифской трепетные лани—
Мелодия, элегия, эвлега . . .
Скрипящая в транцендентальном плане,
Немазанная катится телега.
На Грузию ложится мгла ночная.
В Афинах полночь. В Пятигорске грозы.

. . . И лучше умереть не вспоминая,
Как хороши, как свежи были розы.

To Vladimir Markov

Half-tones of rowan and raspberry
Strewn needlessly in Scotland,
In the melancholy name of Alina,
In the light-blue gold of brass.

Life radiates an astounded smile,
It grows flowers, executes prisoners,
And a guest enters many-columned Corinth,
To exhaust himself in longed-for embraces!

Tremulous does in Scythian traces—
The melody, the elegy, Evlega . . .
An ungreased swaying peasant cart,
Scrapes along its transcendental way.
Night mist descends on Georgia.
Midnight in Athens. Storms in Pyatigorsk.

And better to die without remembering,
How lovely, how fresh were the roses.

Солнце село и краски погасли.
Чист и ясен пустой небосвод.
Как сардинка в оливковом масле,
Одинокая тучка плывет.

Не особенно важная штучка
И, притом, не нужна никому,
Ну, а всё-таки, милая тучка,
Я тебя в это сердце возьму.

Много в нём всевозможного хлама,
Много музыки, мало ума,
И царит в нём Прекрасная Дама,
Кто такая—увидишь сама.

The sun has set and the colors faded.
The empty firmament is clean and clear.
A lonely cloudlet floats along
Like a sardine in olive oil.

Not a particularly important trifle
And, besides, no one needs it,
But, dear little cloud,
I'll take you into my heart anyway.

There is every kind of rubbish there,
Much music, little sense,
In it reigns a Beautiful Lady,
Who is she? You'll have to see for yourself.

Стало тревожно-прохладно,
Благоуханно в саду.
Гром прогремел . . . Ну, и ладно,
Значит, гулять не пойду.

. . . С детства знакомое чувство, —
Чем бы бессмертье купить,
Как бы салазки искусства
К летней грозе прицепить?

In the garden it turned
Fragrant, and threateningly cool.
The thunder thundered . . . Well, OK,
Looks like I won't go for a walk.

A feeling familiar since childhood:
How shall I pay for immortality?
How do I hitch the sleigh of Art
To a summer storm?

Так, занимаясь пустяками—
Покупками или бритьём—
Своими слабыми руками
Мы чудный мир воссоздаём.

И поднимаясь облаками
Ввысь—к небожителям на пир—
Своими слабыми руками
Мы разрушаем этот мир.

Туманные проходят годы,
И вперемежку дышим мы
То затхлым воздухом свободы,
То вольным холодом тюрьмы.

И принимаем вперемежку—
С надменностью встречая их—
То восхищенье, то насмешку
От современников своих.

And so, occupied with trifles,
Daily purchases or shaving,
We re-create a marvelous world
With our own weak hands.

And climbing like clouds
Up and away—where denizens of heaven
Are at feast—we destroy this world
With our own weak hands.

The misty years pass by,
We breathe in in turn,
Now the musty air of freedom,
Now the free chill of prison.

And we accept in turn—
Greeting them with haughtiness—
Now admiration, now ridicule
From our very own contemporaries.

Роману Гулю

Нет в России даже дорогих могил,
Может быть, и были—только я забыл.

Нету Петербурга, Киева, Москвы—
Может быть, и были, да забыл, увы.

Ни границ не знаю, ни морей, ни рек.
Знаю—там остался русский человек.

Русский он по сердцу, русский по уму,
Если я с ним встречусь, я его пойму.

Сразу, с полуслова . . . И тогда начну
Различать в тумане и его страну.

To Roman Gul'

In Russia there aren't even beloved graves,
Maybe once there were, only I've forgotten.

There's no Petersburg, Kiev, Moscow—
Maybe once there were; I've forgotten, alas.

I don't know any borders, seas, or rivers.
I know—that's where Russian man remained.

Russian in his heart, Russian in his mind,
If I meet up with him, I'll understand him.

Right off, from half a word . . . And then I'll
Begin to make out his country in the mist.

Ещё я нахожу очарованье
В случайных мелочах и пустяках —
В романе без конца и без названья,
Вот в этой розе, вянущей в руках.

Мне нравится, что на её муаре
Колышется дождинок серебро,
Что я нашёл её на тротуаре
И выброшу в помойное ведро.

I still find enchantment
When little things and trifles come my way,
In a novel without an ending or a title,
And in this rose, fading here in my hands.

I like that silvery drops of rain
Shimmer on its silky moire,
That I found it on the sidewalk pavement,
And I'll dump it in a garbage pail.

Полу-жалость. Полу-отвращение.
Полу-память. Полу-ощущенье,
Полу-неизвестно что,
Полы моего пальто . . .

Полы моего пальто?
        Так вот в чём дело!

Чуть меня машина не задела
И умчалась вдаль, забрызгав грязью.
Начал вытирать, запачкал руки . . .

Все ещё мне не привыкнуть к скуке,
Скуке мирового безобразья!

Half-compassion, half-revulsion,
Half-memory, half-sensation,
Half-who-knows-what,
The hem of my overcoat . . .

The hem of my overcoat?
         So that's what this is all about!

An automobile almost grazed my body
Then raced away, splattering me with mud.
Started wiping up, got my hands dirty . . .

No, I have yet to get used to boredom,
The boredom of universal ugliness!

Как обидно — чудным даром,
Божьим даром обладать,
Зная, что растратишь даром
Золотую благодать.

И не только зря растратишь,
Жемчуг свиньям раздаря,
Но ещё к нему доплатишь
Жизнь, погубленную зря.

How painful—to possess
A marvelous, God-given gift,
Knowing you'll waste it,
Uselessly, your golden grace.

Not only will you waste it in vain,
Casting pearls before swine,
But to top it all, you'll pay with
Your life, ruined for naught.

Иду — и думаю о разном,
Плету на гроб себе венок,
И в этом мире безобразном
Благообразно одинок.

Но слышу вдруг: война, идея,
Последний бой, двадцатый век . . .
И вспоминаю, холодея,
Что я уже не человек.

А судорога идиота,
Природой созданная зря —
«Урра!» из пасти патриота,
«Долой!» из глотки бунтаря.

I stroll along, thinking of this and that,
Weaving myself a wreath for my tomb,
And in this ugly world
I'm primly and properly alone.

Suddenly I hear: great war, great idea,
The last great fight, the twentieth century . . .
And I recollect, turning cold,
That I am no longer a man.

And the shiver of an idiot,
Created by nature to no purpose—
"Hoooorah!" drops from the patriot's jaw,
"Down with them!" from a rebel's maw.

Свободен путь под Фермопилами
На все четыре стороны.
И Греция цветёт могилами,
Как будто не было войны.

А мы — Леонтьева и Тютчева
Сумбурные ученики —
Мы никогда не знали лучшего,
Чем праздной жизни пустяки.

Мы тешимся самообманами,
И нам потворствует весна,
Пройдя меж трезвыми и пьяными,
Она садится у окна.

«Дыша духами и туманами,
Она садится у окна».
Ей за морями-океанами
Видна блаженная страна:

Стоят рождественские ёлочки,
Скрывая снежную тюрьму.
И голубые комсомолочки,
Визжа, купаются в Крыму.

Они ныряют над могилами,
С одной — стихи, с другой — жених . . .
. . . и Леонид под Фермопилами,
Конечно, умер и за них.

The passage is free at Thermopylae,
In all four directions.
And Greece is blooming with graves,
As if there had been no war.

And we, the confused disciples of
Leontiev and Tiutchev,
We never knew better
Than the trifles of an idle life.

We content ourselves with self-delusions,
Spring panders us along,
Slipping past the sober and the drunk,
She sits down by the window.

"Breathing perfume and mist,
She sits down by the window."
She can discern her blessed country
Beyond the seas and oceans.

There, Christmas trees stand,
Concealing the snowy prison.
And Komsomol girls in blue,
Bathe, squealing with delight, in the Crimea.

They dive over the graves,
One with poems, another with a groom . . .
. . . and Leonidas at Thermopylae,
Of course, he died for them too.

Я хотел бы улыбнуться,
Отдохнуть, домой вернуться . . .
Я хотел бы так немного,
То, что есть почти у всех,
Но что мне просить у Бога—
И бессмыслица, и грех.

I would like to smile,
To rest, to return home . . .
I would like to have so little
Of the things almost everyone has,
But what can I beg of God—
It's all sin and nonsense.

Всё на свете не беда,
Всё на свете ерунда,
Всё на свете прекратится—
И всего верней—проститься,
Дорогие господа,
С этим миром навсегда.

Можно и не умирая,
Оставаясь подлецом,
Нежным мужем и отцом,
Притворяясь и играя,
Быть отличным мертвецом.

All the world's not here nor there,
All the world's just rubbish,
All that is will cease to be,
And it would be best to part ways,
Dear Ladies and Gentlemen,
With this universe forever.

One can, without even dying,
While remaining a scoundrel,
A loving husband and father,
Pretending and playing at it,
Be a perfect corpse.

Я научился понемногу
Шагать со всеми—рядом, в ногу.
По пустякам не волноваться
И правилам повиноваться.

Встают—встаю. Садятся—сяду.
Стозначный помню номер свой.
Лояльно благодарен Аду
За звёздный кров над головой.

I've learned slowly, bit by bit,
To stride in step with everyone.
Not to be bothered by trifles
And to obey the rules.

Everyone stands—stand I. Everyone sits—I sit.
I remember my hundred-digit number.
I'm loyally grateful to Hell
For the starry roof over my head.

Уплывают маленькие ялики
В золотой междупланетный омут.
Вот уже растаял самый маленький,
А за ним и остальные тонут.

На последней самой утлой лодочке
Мы с тобой качаемся вдвоём:
Припасли, дружок, немного водочки,
Вот теперь её и разопьём . . .

Little skiffs float off
Into the golden interplanetary whirlpool.
Already the littlest one has melted away,
And after it the others drown.

We rock together, you and I,
In the last, most wretched little boat:
We put aside, dear friend, a nip of vodka,
So now let's drink it dry . . .

Сознанье, как море, не может молчать,
Стремится сдержаться, не может сдержаться,
Всё рвётся на всё и всему отвечать,
Всему удивляться, на всё раздражаться.

Головокруженье с утра началось,
Всю ночь продолжалось головокруженье,
И вот—долгожданное счастье сбылось:
На миг ослабело Твоё притяженье.

. . . Был синий рассвет. Так блаженно спалось
Так сладко дышалось . . .

                 И вновь началось
Сиянье, волненье, броженье, движенье.

Consciousness, like the sea, cannot remain silent,
It strives to hold back, but it cannot hold back,
It rushes to answer everything and all,
To marvel at all, to be disturbed by everything.

The giddiness began from morning,
The giddiness continued all night,
And here it is: long-awaited happiness came to be,
Your divine pull weakened for an instant.

. . . It was a deep-blue dawn. How blessed was the sleeping,
How sweet was the breathing . . .
                                    And once again there began
Radiance, excitement, agitation, stirring.

Стоят сады в сияньи белоснежном
И ветер шелестит дыханьем влажным.

—Поговорим с тобой о самом важном,
О самом страшном и о самом нежном,
Поговорим с тобой о неизбежном:

Ты прожил жизнь, её не замечая,
Бессмыленно мечтая и скучая—
Вот, наконец, кончается и это . . .

Я слушаю его, не отвечая,
Да он, конечно, и не ждёт ответа.

The orchards stand in the snow-white glow
And the wind rustles with moist breath.

"Let us speak about the most important,
The most horrible and the most tender,
Let us speak about the unavoidable:

You lived your life through, without noticing it,
Thoughtlessly dreaming and growing bored—
Well, finally, that too comes to an end . . ."

I listen to him without answering,
And he, naturally, awaits no answer.

Всё туман. Бреду в тумане я
Скуки и непонимания.
И—с учёным или неучем—
Толковать мне, в общем, не о чем.

Я бы зажил, зажил заново
Не Георгием Ивановым,
А слегка очеловеченным,
Энергичным, щёткой вымытым,
Вовсе роком не отмеченным,
Первым встречным-поперечным—
Всё равно какое имя там . . .

It's all a fog. I wander about in a fog
Of boredom and misunderstanding.
And—with the learned or the ignorant—
For me, in general, there's nothing to discuss.

I'd begin to live, to live again
Not as Georgy Ivanov,
But as someone slightly humanized
Energetic, scrubbed with a brush,
Not marked at all by fate,
A hale fellow well met—
And to hell with the name . . .

> В Петербурге мы сойдёмся снова,
> Словно солнце мы похоронили в нём . . .
>
> *О. Мандельштам*

Четверть века прошло за границей,
И надеяться стало смешным.
Лучезарное небо над Ниццей
Навсегда стало небом родным.
Тишина благодатного юга,
Шорох волн, золотое вино . . .

Но поёт петербургская вьюга
В занесённое снегом окно,
Что пророчество мёртвого друга
Обязательно сбыться должно.

> In Petersburg we'll come together again,
> As if we buried the sun there . . .
> *Osip Mandelstam*

A quarter-century passed abroad
And to hope has become absurd.
The radiant sky over Nice
Became our native sky forever.
The quiet of the blessed south,
The splash of waves, the golden wine . . .

But a Petersburg storm sings
In a snow-drifted window
That the prophecy of a dead friend
Surely must come true.

Эти сумерки вечерние
Вспомнил я по воле случая.
Плыли в Костромской губернии,
Тишина, благополучие.

Празднично цвела природа,
Словно ей обновку сшили:
Груши грузными корзинами,
Астры пышными охапками . . .
(В чайной «русского народа»
Трезвенники спирт глушили:
—Внутренного—жарь резинами!
—Немца—закидаем шапками!)

И на грани кругозора,
Сквозь дремоту палисадников,—
Силуэты чёрных всадников
С красным знаменем позора.

I recalled those twilight evenings
By force of circumstance:
Once idleness, abundance
Wafted over Kostroma province.

Nature bloomed in holiday array,
As if sporting a new outfit:
Heavy basketfuls of pears,
Asters in magnificent armfuls . . .
(In the tearoom of "The Black Hundreds"
The abstinent ones sopped up the alcohol:
"The internal enemy—we'll let 'em have it!
The Germans—we'll just bury 'em!")

And at the edge of the horizon,
Through the sleepiness of front gardens,
Silhouettes of Dark Riders
Carrying the red banner of shame.

Овеянный тускнеющею славой,
В кольце святош, кретинов и пройдох,
Не изнемог в бою Орёл Двуглавый,
А жутко, унизительно издох.

Один сказал с усмешкою: «Дождался!»
Другой заплакал: «Господи, прости . . .»
А чучела никто не догадался
В изгнанье, как в могилу, унести.

Beclouded by lackluster glory,
Encircled by hypocrites, cretins, and scoundrels,
Two-Headed Eagle, not exhausted in the battle,
But horribly, humiliatingly gave up the ghost.

Someone said with a smirk: "He got his!"
Someone began to cry: "Lord Almighty, have mercy . . ."
But no one thought to carry off into exile
The dummy, as if to its grave.

Голубая речка
Зябкая волна,
Времени утечка
Явственно слышна.

Голубая речка
Предлагает мне
Тёплое местечко
На холодном дне.

Sky-blue rivulet
Chilly wave,
Time's flowing pet
Clearly hears the grave.

Sky-blue rivulet
Offers me
A cushy corner seat
Cold bottom of the sea.

Луны начищенный пятак
Блеснул сквозь паутину веток,
Речное озаряя дно.

И лодка — повернувшись так,
Не может повернуться этак,
Раз всё вперёд предрешено.

А если не предрешено?
Тогда . . . И я могу проснуться —
(О, только разбуди меня!),

Широко распахнуть окно
И благодарно улыбнуться
Сиянью завтрашнего дня.

The moon's shining five-kopeck coin
Flashed through a spiderweb of branches,
Illuminating the river bottom.

And a boat—turning thus
Cannot turn any other way,
Since everything is preordained.

But if not preordained?
Then . . . I can awaken—
(Oh, only be sure to wake me!)

I can throw the window open wide
And smile gratefully
At the radiance of the coming day.

Звёзды меркли в бледнеющем небе,
Всё слабей отражаясь в воде.
Облака проплывали, как лебеди,
С розовеющей далью редея . . .

Лебедями проплыли сомнения
И тревога в сияньи померкла,
Без следа растворившись в душе,

И глядела душа, хорошея,
Как влюблённая женщина в зеркало,
В торжество, неизвестное мне.

The stars faded in the paling sky,
Ever weaker, reflected in the water.
Clouds floated by, like swans,
Thinning into the rosy distance . . .

Doubts floated by like swans
And disquiet faded in the radiance,
Dissolving without a trace in the soul,

And the soul gazed, growing lovely,
Like a woman in love in her mirror,
Into triumph, one unknown to me.

Белая лошадь бредёт без упряжки.
Белая лошадь, куда ты бредёшь?
Солнце сияет. Платки и рубашки
Треплет в саду предвесенняя дрожь.

Я, что когда-то с Россией простился
(Ночью навстречу полярной заре),
Не оглянулся, не перекрестился
И не заметил, как вдруг очутился
В этой глухой европейской дыре.

Хоть поскучать бы . . . Но я не скучаю.
Жизнь потерял, а покой берегу.
Письма от мёртвых друзей получаю
И, прочитав, с облегчением жгу
На голубом предвесеннем снегу.

A white horse roams without a harness.
White horse, where are you headed?
The sun shines. A spring-prelude shiver
Tosses kerchiefs and shirts in the garden.

I, who some time ago parted from Russia
(At night to meet the polar dawn),
I didn't look back, didn't cross myself
And didn't notice how I'd suddenly landed
In this dreary European hole.

If only I had something to long for . . . But I don't.
I lost my life, but I guard my peace.
I receive letters from dead friends
And having read them through, I burn them with relief
On the sky-blue spring-prelude snow.

Нечего тебе тревожиться,
Надо бы давно простить.
Но чудак грустит и бóжится,
Что не может не грустить.

Нам бы, да в сияньи шёлковом,
Осень-вёсен поджидая,
На Успенском или Волковом,
Под песочком Голодая,
На ступенях Исаакия
Или в прорубь на Неве . . .

. . . Беспокойство. Ну, и всякие
Вожделенья в голове.

There is no reason for you to worry,
You should have forgiven long ago.
But this odd fellow is sad and swears to God
That he cannot help being sad.

We should go, in a silky radiance
Awaiting our autumn-spring,
To the Uspensky or Volkov Cemetery,
Below the sands of Golodai,
On the steps of St. Isaac's
Or into an ice-hole in the Neva . . .

The worry. And yes, all those
Temptations in your head.

Цветущих яблонь тень сквозная,
Косого солнца бледный свет,
И снова—ничего не зная—
Как в пять или в пятнадцать лет,—

Замученное сердце радо
Тому, что я домой бреду,
Тому, что нежная прохлада
Разлита в яблонном саду.

The transparent shade of apple blossoms,
The pale light of the slanting sun
And once again—knowing nothing—
As though you were five or fifteen—

The tortured heart is glad
That I'm wandering my way home,
That a tender coolness
Floods the apple orchard.

Тускнеющий вечерний час,
Река и частокол в тумане . . .
Что связывает нас? Всех нас?—
Взаимное непониманье.

Все наши беды и дела,
Жизнь всех людей без исключенья . . .
Века, века она текла
И вот я принесён теченьем—

В парижский пригород, сюда,
Где мальчик огород копает,
Гудят протяжно провода
И робко первая звезда
Сквозь светлый сумрак проступает.

The dimming evening hour,
The river and the stake fence in the mist . . .
What binds us together, all of us?
Mutual misunderstanding.

All our misfortunes and endeavors,
The life of all people without exception
Has streamed past for ages upon ages
And now I am brought by that flow—

Here, to a Paris suburb,
Where a boy digs in the garden patch,
Where wires whine long and loud
And the first star shyly
Shows through the shimmering twilight.

На границе снега и таянья,
Неподвижности и движения,
Легкомыслия и отчаяния—
Сердцебиение, головокружение . . .

Голубая ночь одиночества—
На осколки жизнь разбивается,
Исчезают имя и отчество,
И фамилия расплывается . . .

Точно звёзды, встают пророчества,
Обрываются! . . Не сбываются! . .

On the border of snow and melt,
Of immobility and movement,
Of nonchalance and despair—
A beating heart, a spinning head . . .

The pale-blue night of solitude—
Life breaks into shards,
Your name and patronymic disappear,
Your family name grows blurry . . .

Quite like stars, prophesies arise,
Torn loose, they come to nothing.

Закат в полнеба занесён,
Уходит в пурпур и виссон
Лазурно-кружевная Ницца . . .

. . . Леноре снится страшный сон—
Леноре ничего не снится.

The sunset ranges half the sky,
Azure-filigreed Nice
Recedes to purple and fine linen . . .

Lenore dreams a dreadful dream—
Lenore dreams nothing.

Я твёрдо решился и тут же забыл,
На что я так твёрдо решился.
День влажно-сиренево-солнечный был
И этим вопрос разрешился.

Так часто бывает: куда-то спешу
И в трепете света и тени
Сначала раскаюсь, потом согрешу
И строчка за строчкой навек запишу
Благоуханье сирени.

I firmly decided and right then forgot
What I had so firmly decided.
It was a lilac-moist-sunny day
And with that the issue resolved.

It often happens: I hurry somewhere
And in the flickering of light and shade,
At first I repent, then I sin
And line after line I write down for all time
The fragrance of lilac.

Насладись, пока не поздно,
Ведь искать недалеко,
Тем, что в мире грациозно,
Грациозно и легко.

Больше нечему учиться,
Прозевал и был таков:
Пара медных пятаков,
«Без речей и без венков»
(Иль с речами — как случится).

Take pleasure, before it is too late,
You can find it close at hand,
In what is graceful in this world,
Graceful and light.

You've nothing more to study,
Missed out and gone in a flash:
A pair of five-kopeck copper pieces,
"Without speeches and wreathes"
(Or with speeches—whatever happens).

Поэзия: искусственная поза,
Условное сиянье звёздных чар,
Где улыбаясь произносят — «Роза»
И с содраганьем думают — «Анчар».

Где, говоря о рае, дышат адом
Мучительных ночей и страшных дней,
Пропитанных насквозь блаженным ядом,
Проросших в мироздание корней.

Poetry: an artificial pose,
A conventional shining of astral charms,
Where, smiling, they say—"The Rose"
And with a shudder think—"The Upas Tree."

Where, speaking of paradise, they inhale the hell
Of torturous nights and terrible days
Saturated through with the blessed poison
Of roots overgrowing into the universal order.

Мне весна ничего не сказала—
Не могла. Может быть—не нашлась.
Только в мутном пролёте вокзала
Мимолетная люстра зажглась.

Только кто-то кому-то с перрона
Поклонился в ночной синеве,
Только слабо блеснула корона
На несчастной моей голове.

Spring said nothing to me—
It could not. Perhaps it didn't find the words.
Only in the turbid vault of the train station
A fugitive chandelier flashed into light.

Only from the platform someone bowed
To someone else in the blue night haze,
Only the crown shone weakly
On my unhappy head.

Почти не видно человека среди сиянья и шелков—
Галантнейший художник века, галантнейшего из веков.

Гармония? Очарованье? Разуверенье? Всё не то.
Никто не подыскал названья прозрачной прелести Ватто.

Как роза вянущая в вазе (зачем Господь её сорвал?),
Как русский Демон на Кавказе, он в Валансьене тосковал . . .

A man is almost lost midst radiance and silks—
Such is the work of the courtliest artist of the courtliest of epochs.

Harmony? Enchantment? Disillusionment? None of those.
No one found a name for the transparent loveliness of Watteau.

As a rose wilting in a vase (why did God pluck it?),
As a Russian Demon in the Caucasus, he was miserable in Valenciennes.

Ветер с Невы. Леденеющий март.
Площадь. Дворец. Часовые. Штандарт.

. . . Как я завидовал вам, обыватели,
Обыкновенные люди простые:
Богоискатели, бомбометатели,
В этом дворце, в Чухломе ль, в каземате ли
Снились вам, в сущности, сны золотые . . .

В чёрной шинели, с погонами синими,
Шёл я, не видя ни улиц, ни лиц.
Видя, как звёзды встают над пустынями
Ваших волнений и ваших столиц.

Wind from the Neva. Freezing March.
The Square. The Palace. Sentries. The Imperial Colors.

How I envied you, you regular folk,
Ordinary, simple people:
God-seekers, bomb-throwers,
In this Palace, in Chukhloma or in jail,
You dreamed, in essence, golden dreams . . .

In a black trench coat with blue shoulder straps,
I walked on, not seeing streets or faces.
Seeing how stars rise over the deserts
Of your disturbances and your capital cities.

Просил. Но никто не помог.
Хотел помолиться. Не мог.
Вернулся домой. Ну, пора!
Не ждать же ещё до утра.

И вспомнил несчастный дурак,
Пощупав, крепка ли петля,
С отчаяньем прыгая в мрак,
Не то, чем прекрасна земля,
А грязный московский кабак,
Лакея засаленный фрак,
Гармошки заливистый вздор,
Огарок свечи, корридор,
На дверце два белых нуля.

He pleaded, but no one helped.
He wanted to pray a bit. He could not.
He returned home. Well, it's time!
Really no use waiting for the morning.

And he remembered—the unlucky fool,
Probing to see if the noose held firm,
In despair leaping into the dark—
Not that which makes the world splendid,
But a filthy Moscow tavern,
A flunky's greasy coat,
A concertina's wailing gibberish,
A candle butt, a corridor,
And two white zeroes on the little door.

Бредёт старик на рыбный рынок
Купить полфунта судака.
Блестят мимозы от дождинок,
Блестит зеркальная река.

Провинциальные жилища.
Туземный говор. Лай собак.
Всё на земле — питьё и пища,
Кровать и крыша. И табак.

Даль. Облака. Вот это — ангел,
Другое — словно водолаз,
А третье — совершенный Врангель,
Моноклем округливший глаз.

Но Врангель, это в Петрограде,
Стихи, шампанское, снега . . .
О, пожалейте, Бога ради:
Склероз в крови, болит нога.

Никто его не пожалеет
И не за что его жалеть.
Старик скрипучий околеет,
Как всем придется околеть.

Но всё-таки . . . А остальное,
Что мне дано ещё, пока —
Сады цветущею весною,
Мистраль, полфунта судака?

An old man plods to the fish market
To buy a half-pound of perch.
Mimosas shine with raindrops,
The river shines, mirror-like.

Provincial dwellings.
Foreign chatter. Dogs' barking.
Everything on this earth is drink and food,
A bed and a roof. And a smoke.

The distance. Clouds. That one's an angel,
That other—like a Newfoundland dog,
A third—the spitting image of Wrangel,
A monocle circling his eye.

But Wrangel, that's in Petrograd,
Poetry, champagne, snows . . .
Oh, have pity, for God's sake,
Sclerosis in the blood, an aching leg.

No one will have pity on him
And there's nothing to pity him for.
This creaky old man will drop,
Like everyone must drop dead.

But all the same . . . How about the rest
That is still given to me, for now—
The gardens in spring bloom,
The mistral, the half-pound of perch?

Жизнь пришла в порядок
В золотом покое.
На припёке грядок
Нежатся левкои.

Белые, лиловые
И вчера, и завтра.
В солнечной столовой
Накрывают завтрак.

. . . В озере купаться
—Как светла вода!—
И не просыпаться
Больше никогда.

Life has come together
In golden peace.
Gillyflowers bask tenderly,
Their beds drenched in the sun.

White, lily-hued,
Like yesterday and like tomorrow.
In the sunlit dining room
Breakfast will be served.

To take a dip in the lake—
The water is so bright!
And never awaken
Ever again.

Меняется прическа и костюм,
Но остается тем же наше тело,
Надежды, страсти, беспокойный ум,
Чья б воля изменить их ни хотела.

Слепой Гомер и нынешний поэт,
Безвестный, обездоленный изгнаньем,
Хранят один — неугасимый! — свет,
Владеют тем же драгоценным знаньем.

И черни, требующей новизны,
Он говорит: «Нет новизны. Есть мера,
А вы мне отвратительно-смешны,
Как варвар, критикующий Гомера!»

Dress and hairstyles change,
But our body, hopes, passions,
Restless mind stay the same,
No matter whose wish it is to change them.

Blind Homer and today's poet,
Unknown, bereaved by exile,
They both keep one—unquenchable!—light,
Possessing that same precious knowledge!

And to the mob that demands novelty,
He says: "There is no novelty. There is measure,
And you are obscenely ridiculous to me,
Like a barbarian who criticizes Homer!"

Волны шумели: «Скорее, скорее!»
К гибели лёгкую лодку несли,
Голубоватые стебли порея
В красный туман прорастали с земли.

Горы дымились, валежником тлея,
И настигали их с разных сторон, —
Лунное имя твое, Лорелея,
Рейнская полночь твоих похорон.

. . . Вот я иду по осеннему саду
И папиросу несу, как свечу.
Вот на скамейку чугунную сяду,
Брошу окурок. Ногой растопчу.

The waves called: "Faster, faster!"
Carrying the light boat to destruction;
The leek's bluish stems sprouted
From the ground into the red fog.

Mountains wafted smoke, fallen branches smoldering,
Overtaken from all sides
By your lunar name, Lorelei,
By the Rhine midnight of your funeral.

Now I walk about the autumn garden
Carrying a cigarette like a candle.
Now I sit on a cast-iron bench.
I throw away the butt. I crush it with my foot.

Я люблю безнадежный покой,
В октябре — хризантемы в цвету,
Огоньки за туманной рекой,
Догоревшей зари нищету . . .

Тишину безымянных могил,
Все банальности «Песен без слов»,
То, что Анненский жадно любил,
То, чего не терпел Гумилёв.

I love hopeless peace,
October—chrysanthemums in bloom,
Twinkling lights beyond the misty river,
The poverty of a declining sunset . . .

The quiet of nameless graves,
All the banalities of *Songs Without Words*,
That which Annensky greedily loved,
That which Gumilyov could not abide.

О, нет, не обращаюсь к миру я
И вашего не жду признания.
Я попросту хлороформирую
Поэзией своё сознание.

И наблюдаю с безучастием,
Как растворяются сомнения,
Как боль сливается со счастием
В сияньи одеревенения.

No, I don't speak to the world
Nor wait for your acknowledgment.
I simply chloroform
My consciousness with poetry.

And I observe with apathy,
How doubts dissolve,
How pain merges with happiness
In a glow of stupefaction.

Если бы я мог забыться,
Если бы, что так устало,
Перестало сердце биться,
Сердце биться перестало,

Наконец — угомонилось,
Навсегда окаменело,
Но — как Лермонтову снилось —
Чтобы где-то жизнь звенела . . .

. . . Что любил, что не допето,
Что уже не видно взглядом,
Чтобы было близко где-то,
Где-то близко было рядом . . .

If only I could sink into oblivion,
If only my so weary heart,
Stopped beating,
My heart stopped beating,

At last knowing peace,
Grew stone-still forever,
But as Lermontov dreamed,
Let life ring out somewhere . . .

What I loved, what was left unsung,
What vision already cannot see,
Let it be somewhere close,
Somewhere close and next to me . . .

Мне больше не страшно. Мне томно.
Я медленно в пропасть лечу
И вашей России не помню
И помнить её не хочу.

И не отзываются дрожью
Банальной и сладкой тоски
Поля с колосящейся рожью,
Берёзки, дымки, огоньки . . .

I'm not afraid anymore. I'm listless.
I slowly fly into the abyss
And I don't remember your Russia
And I don't want to remember it.

And they don't call forth the shivering
Of banal and sugary pangs of longing,
Those fields of flowering rye,
Slender birches, puffs of smoke, twinkling lights.

То, что было, и то, чего не было,
То, что ждали мы, то, что не ждём,
Просияло в весеннее небо,
Прошумело коротким дождём.

Это всё. Ничего не случилось.
Жизнь, как прежде, идёт не спеша.
И напрасно в сиянье просилась,
В эти четверть минуты душа.

What has been, and what never was,
What we waited for, what we do not expect,
It all flashed in the spring sky,
Rang out like a short rain.

That is all. Nothing happened.
Life, as before, goes on unhurriedly.
And during those fifteen seconds
In vain the soul begged release into radiance.

Чем дольше живу я, тем менее
Мне ясно, чего я хочу.
Купил бы, пожалуй, имение.
Да чем за него заплачу?
Порою мечтаю прославиться
И тут же над этим смеюсь,
Непрочь и «подальше» отправиться,
И всё же боюсь. Сознаюсь . . .

The longer I live, the less
Clear it is to me what I want.
Perhaps I could buy an estate.
But how would I pay for it?
At times I dream of becoming famous,
And right away I laugh at it,
I'm not against "crossing over" either,
But still I'm afraid. I admit it.

Всё на свете дело случая —
Вот нажму на лотерею,
Денег выиграю кучу я
И усы, конечно, сбрею.

Потому что — для чего же
Богачу нужны усы?
Много, милостивый Боже,
В мире покупной красы:
И нилоны, и часы,
И вещички подороже.

In this world everything is a matter of chance—
I'll punch my lottery ticket
I'll win a pile of money
And, of course, I'll shave my mustache.

Because what use anyway
Does a rich man have for a mustache?
Merciful God, there's so much
Bought beauty in the world:
Nylons and watches,
And other more expensive gewgaws.

Здесь в лесах даже розы цветут,
Даже пальмы растут — вот умора!
Но как странно — во Франции, тут,
Я нигде не встречал мухомора.

Может быть, просто климат не тот —
Мало сосен, берёзок, болотца . . .
Ну, а может быть, он не растёт,
Потому что ему не растётся

С той поры, с той далёкой поры —
. . . Чахлый ельник, Балтийское море,
Тишина, пустота, комары,
Чья-то кровь на кривом мухоморе . . .

Here in the forests even roses bloom,
Even palm trees grow—what a crazy joke!
But how strange—here, in France,
Nowhere have I come upon a toadstool.

Maybe it's simply not the right climate—
Too few pines, birches, and forest bogs . . .
Or maybe it doesn't grow
Simply because it doesn't feel like it

Since that time, since that distant time—
. . . A stunted fir grove, the Baltic Sea,
Silence, emptiness, mosquitoes,
Someone's blood on a crooked toadstool . . .

Не станет ни Европы, ни Америки,
Ни Царскосельских парков, ни Москвы—
Припадок атомической истерики
Всё распылит в сияньи синевы.

Потом над миром ласково протянется
Прозрачный, всепрощающий дымок . . .
И Тот, кто мог помочь и не помог,
В предвечном одиночестве останется.

Gone will be Europe and America,
Moscow and the parks of Tsarskoe Selo—
An attack of atomic hysterics will
Pulverize everything in the shining blue.

Then above the world will tenderly stretch out
A transparent, all-forgiving smoke . . .
And He, who could have helped but did not,
Will remain in solitude everlasting.

Всё на свете пропадает даром,
Что же Ты робеешь? Не робей!
Размозжи его одним ударом,
На осколки звёздные разбей!

Отрави его горчичным газом
Или бомбами испепели—
Что угодно—только кончи разом
С мукою и музыкой земли!

All in this world is lost uselessly,
Why doest Thou shy away? Don't be shy!
Blast it to nothing with one blow,
Bust it into starry shards!

Poison it with mustard gas
Or incinerate it with bombs—
With whatever—only be done once and for all
With the torment and the music of this earth!

Листья падали, падали, падали
И никто им не мог помешать . . .
От гниющих цветов, как от падали,
Тяжело становилось дышать.

И неслось светозарное пение
Над плескавшей в тумане рекой.
Обещая в блаженном успении
Отвратительный вечный покой.

The leaves fell, and fell, and fell
And no one could stop them . . .
It became difficult to breathe
From the rotting flowers, rotting like carrion.

And radiant singing wafted
Over a splashing river in the mist,
Promising in blessed dormition
Loathsome eternal rest.

Ну, мало ли что бывает?
Мало ли что бывало—
Вот облако проплывает,
Проплывает, как проплывало,

Деревья, автомобили,
Лягушки в пруду поют,
 . . . Сегодня меня убили,
Завтра тебя убьют.

Well, anything can happen!
Everything has happened—
Now a cloud floats by,
Floats by, like it once floated by,

Trees, motorcars,
Frogs singing in a pond . . .
. . . Today I got killed,
Tomorrow you'll get killed.

Всё представляю в блаженном тумане я:
Статуи, арки, сады, цветники.
Тёмные волны прекрасной реки . . .

Раз начинаются воспоминания,
Значит . . . А может быть, всё пустяки.

. . .Вот вылезаю, как зверь из берлоги я,
В холод Парижа, сутулый, больной . . .
«Бедные люди» — пример тавтологии,
Кем это сказано? Может быть, мной.

I conjure it all in a blessed mist:
Statues, archways, gardens, and flower beds.
Dark waves of the magnificent river . . .

Once the memories begin,
That means . . . But maybe it's all nothing.

Now, like an animal, I crawl out of my lair
Into the cold of Paris, stooped, sick . . .
Poor Folk—an example of a tautology,
Who said that? Perhaps it was me.

Не обманывают только сны.
Сон всегда освобожденье: мы
Тайно, безнадежно влюблены
В рай за стенами своей тюрьмы.

Мильонеру — снится нищета.
Оборванцу — золото рекой.
Мне — моя последняя мечта,
Неосуществимая — покой.

Only dreams do not deceive.
A dream is always liberation:
We, secretly, hopelessly are enamored
Of the paradise beyond our prison walls.

A millionaire—he dreams of poverty.
A bum in rags—he dreams of a river of gold.
I dream my final, unrealizable
Dream—I dream of peace.

На юге Франции прекрасны
Альпийский холод, нежный зной.
Шипит суглинок желто-красный
Под аметистовой волной.
И дети, крабов собирая,
Смеясь медузам и волнам,
Подходят к самой двери рая,
Который только снится нам.

Сверкает звёздами браслета
Прохлады лунная рука
И фиолетовое лето
Нам обеспечено — пока
В лучах расцвета-увяданья,
В узоре пены и плюща
Сияет вечное страданье,
Крылами чаек трепеща.

In the south of France so fine
Alpine cold, and tender heat,
Where the loam sizzles yellow-red
Beneath an amethystine wave.
And the children, gathering crabs,
Laughing at the jellyfish and waves,
Approach the very door to paradise,
Of which we can only dream.

The moonlit hand of coolness
Gleams with a starry bracelet,
And violet summer
Assured to us—so long as
In rays of dawn-decay,
In a filigree of foam and ivy
Eternal suffering shines,
Flicking the wings of gulls.

Т. Г. Терентьевой

А ещё недавно было всё, что надо —
Липы и дорожки векового сада,
Там грустил Тургенев . . .
                Было всё, что надо,
Белые коллоны, кабинет и зала —
Там грустил Тургенев . . .

            И ему казалась
Жизнь стихотвореньем, музыкой, пастелью,
Где, не грея, светит мировая слава,
Где ещё не скоро сменится метелью
Золотая осень крепостного права.

to Tatiana Terentieva

Not so long ago we had everything—
Linden trees and paths in the age-old garden,
Where Turgenev pined . . .
                    We had everything,
White columns, the study and drawing room—
Where Turgenev pined . . .

            And to him
Life seemed a poem, music, a pastel drawing,
Where, without warning, worldwide fame shines,
Where a snowstorm will not soon replace
The golden autumn of serfdom.

—Когда-нибудь, когда устанешь ты,
Устанешь до последнего предела . . .
—Но я и так устал до тошноты,
До отвращения . . .
                              —Тогда, другое дело.
Тогда—спокойно, не спеша проверь
Все мысли, все дела, все ощущенья,
И, если перевесит отвращенье—

Завидую тебе: перед тобою дверь
Распахнута в восторг развоплощенья.

"Sometime, when you grow weary,
When you grow weary to the utmost limit . . ."
"But I am already weary to nausea,
To loathing . . ."
                    "Well then, that's all right.
Then—calmly, unhurriedly examine
All your thoughts, deeds, all your sensations,
And if your loathing outweighs them—

I envy you: before you is a door,
Flung open to the rapture of disincarnation."

Мы не молоды. Но и не стары.
Мы не мёртвые. И не живые.
Вот мы слушаем рокот гитары
И романса «слова роковые».

О беспамятном счастье цыганском,
Об угарной любви и разлуке,
И — как вызов — стаканы с шампанским
Подымают дрожащие руки.

За бессмыслицу! За неудачи!
За потерю всего дорогого!
И за то, что могло быть иначе,
И за то — что не надо другого!

We are not young, yet neither are we old.
We are not dead, but we're not living, either.
Now we are listening to the guitar's murmur,
And to a love song's "fateful words."

About delirious gypsy happiness,
About frenzied love and parting,
And—like a challenge—glasses of champagne,
Raised by trembling hands.

To senselessness! To misfortunes!
To the loss of all that's dear!
And to what could have been otherwise,
And to our needing nothing else!

Как всё бесцветно, всё безвкусно,
Мертво внутри, смешно извне,
Как мне невыразимо грустно,
Как тошнотворно скучно мне . . .

Зевая сам от этой темы,
Её меняю на ходу.

—Смотри, как пышны хризантемы
В сожжённом осенью саду —
Как будто лермонтовский Демон
Грустит в оранжевом аду,
Как будто вспоминает Врубель
Обрывки творческого сна
И царственно идёт на убыль
Лиловой музыки волна . . .

How all is colorless, and tasteless,
Dead inside, ridiculous outside,
How I am intolerably sad,
How nauseatingly bored I am . . .

Myself yawning from this theme,
I change it mid-stride:

"Look how luxuriant the chrysanthemums
In the garden scorched by the autumn—
As if Lermontov's Demon
Is grieving in an orange hell,
As if Vrubel remembers
Snatches of a creative dream
And the wave of lilac music
Regally goes into decline . . ."

И разве мог бы я, о посуди сама,
В твои глаза взглянуть и не сойти с ума.

«Сады» (1921)

1

И.О.

Ты не расслышала, а я не повторил.
Был Петербург, апрель, закатный час,
Сиянье, волны, каменные львы . . .
И ветерок с Невы
Договорил за нас.

Ты улыбалась. Ты не поняла,
Что будет с нами, что нас ждёт.
Черёмуха в твоих руках цвела . . .
Вот наша жизнь прошла,
А это не пройдёт.

And could I, O judge for yourself,
Look into your eyes and not lose my mind.

Gardens (1921)

1

To Irina Odoevtseva

You didn't make it out, I did not repeat.
Once there was Petersburg, April, the sunset hour,
The radiance, the waves, the lions of stone . . .
     And a light breeze from the Neva
     Finished what we had to say.

You smiled. You didn't understand,
What would become of us, what would await us.
A cherry sprig blossomed in your hands . . .
Thus our life has passed,
But this shall not.

2

И.О.

Распылённый мильоном мельчайших частиц
В ледяном, безвоздушном, бездушном эфире,
Где ни солнца, ни звёзд, ни деревьев, ни птиц,
Я вернусь — отраженьем — в потерянном мире.

И опять, в романтическом Летнем Саду,
В голубой белизне петербургского мая,
По пустынным аллеям неслышно пройду,
Драгоценные плечи твои обнимая.

2

To Irina Odoevtseva

Ground to a million miniscule particles
In the icy, airless, soulless ether,
Where there are no sun, no stars, no trees, no birds,
I will come again, reflection-like, to a lost world.

And again, in the romantic Summer Garden,
In the pale-blue whiteness of a Petersburg May,
I'll walk unheard along the empty alleyways,
Embracing your precious shoulders.

И.О.

Вся сиянье, вся непостоянство,
Как осколок погибшей звезды—
Ты заброшена в наше пространство,
Где тебе даже звёзды чужды.

И летишь—в никуда, ниоткуда—
Обречённая вечно грустить,
Отрицать невозможное чудо
И бояться его пропустить.

3

To Irina Odoevtseva

All radiance, all inconstancy,
Like the shard of a perished star—
You're thrown into our space,
Where even stars are alien to you.

And you fly into nowhere, from nowhere,
Condemned to pine forever,
To reject the impossible miracle,
And to be afraid to let it pass you by.

4

И.О.

Отзовись, кукушечка, яблочко, змеёныш,
Весточка, царапинка, снежинка, ручеёк.
Нежности последыш, нелепости приёмыш,
Кофе-чае-сахарный потерянный паёк.

Отзовись, очухайся, пошевелись спросонок,
В одеяльной одури, в подушечной глуши,
Белочка, метёлочка, косточка, утёнок,
Ленточкой, верёвочкой, чулочком задуши.

Отзовись, пожалуйста. Да, нет — не отзовётся.
Ну и делать нечего. Проживём и так.
Из огня да в полымя. Где тонко, там и рвётся.
Палочка-стукалочка, полушка-четвертак.

4

To Irina Odoevtseva

Say something, my cuckoo, little apple, baby snake,
Bit-o'-news, scratchums, snowflake, and rivulet.
Youngest one of tenderness, adopted from absurd,
The sugar-coffee-tea ration, lost.

Say something, come to yourself, stir in your sleep,
In blanketed silliness, in pillowed depths;
Squirrelette, broomikins, fruit pit, and duckling,
Strangle me with a ribbon, a bit of string, a stocking.

Say something, please. No—she won't say anything.
Well, nothing for it. I'll manage all the same.
From the fire into the frying pan. The weakest link.
A drumstick, a quarter, a twenty-five-kopeck piece.

... Мне всегда открывается та же
Залитая чернилом страница ...

И. Анненский

И.О.

Может быть, умру я в Ницце,
Может быть, умру в Париже,
Может быть, в моей стране.
Для чего же о странице
Неизбежной, чёрно-рыжей
Постоянно думать мне!

В голубом дыханьи моря,
В ледяных стаканах пива
(Тех, что мы сейчас допьём) —
Пена счастья — волны горя,
Над могилами крапива,
Штора на окне твоём.

Вот её колышет воздух
И из комнаты уносит
Наше зыбкое тепло,
То, что растворится в звёздах,
То, о чём никто не спросит,
То, что было и прошло.

. . . I always chance to open that same
Page, awash in ink . . .
Innokenty Annensky

To Irina Odoevtseva

Perhaps I shall die in Nice,
Perhaps in Paris,
Perhaps in my own country.
Why do I constantly
Think about that page,
Unavoidable, darkly ruddy!

In the sky-blue breathing of the sea,
In the iced glasses of beer
(The ones we'll drink up now)—
The foam of happiness—the waves of woe,
Stinging nettles over the graves,
The drapery on your window.

Now a breath of air ruffles it,
Carrying away from the room
Our fragile warmth,
That will dissolve in the stars,
That no one will inquire about,
That once was and now is gone.

Зима идёт своим порядком —
Опять снежок. Ещё должок.
И гадко в этом мире гадком
Жевать вчерашний пирожок.

И в этом мире слишком узком,
Где всё потеря и урон
Считать себя с чего-то русским,
Читать стихи, считать ворон,

Разнежась, радоваться маю,
Когда растаяла зима . . .
О, Гоподи, не понимаю,
Как все мы, не сойдя с ума,

Встаём-ложимся, щёки бреем,
Гуляем или пьём-едим,
О прошлом-будущем жалеем,
А душу всё не продадим.

Вот эту вянущую душку —
За гривенник, копейку, грош.
Дороговато? — За полушку.
Бери бесплатно! — Не берёшь?

Winter goes along its usual way—
Again light snow. Still deeper in debt.
It's revolting in this revolting world
To chew on yesterday's dumpling.

And in this too narrow world,
Where all is loss and casualty
To consider oneself for some reason Russian,
To read poems, to idle away the time,

Feeling tender, to find joy in May,
When winter melted . . .
Oh, dear God, I don't understand,
How we all haven't lost our minds,

Get up, lie down, shave our cheeks,
Walk around or drink and eat,
Regret the past and future,
And haven't sold our souls yet.

This waning petty soul—
For a farthing, a kopeck, a penny.
Too much? For a ha'penny?
Take it for free! You won't take it?!

Скучно, скучно мне до одуренья!
Скушал бы клубничного варенья,
Да потом меня изжога съест.

Хоть в раю у Бога много мест,
Только все расписаны заране.

Мне бы прогреметь на барабане,
Проскакать на золотом баране,
Позевать на Индию в окно.
Мне бы рыбкой в море-океане
Сигануть на мировое дно!

Скучно от несбыточных желаний . . .
. . . Вечный сон: забор, на нём слова.
Любопытно — поглядим-ка.
Заглянул. А там трава, дрова.
Вьётся та же скука-невидимка.

I'm bored, bored silly!
I'd savor some strawberry jam,
No, heartburn will eat me up later.

To be sure, God has plenty of places in paradise,
Only they're all assigned ahead of time.

I'd like to thunder away on a drum,
Gallop by on a golden ram,
Yawn through my window at India.
If only I could be a little fish in the ocean-sea,
Diving down to the bottom of the world!

I'm bored by desires that never come to be . . .
An eternal dream: a fence, some words on it.
That's curious—let's have a look.
I peeked inside. In there only grass and logs.
The same invisible boredom circles round.

Накипевшая за годы
Злость, сводящая с ума,
Злость к поборникам свободы,
Злость к ревнителям ярма,
Злость к хамью и джентльменам —
Разномастным специменам
Той же «мудрости земной»,
К миру и стране родной.

Злость? Вернее, безразличье
К жизни, к вечности, к судьбе.
Нечто кошкино иль птичье,
Отчего не по себе
Верным рыцарям приличья,
Благонравным А и Б,
Что уселись на трубе.

Building up for years,
Fury that drives you crazy,
Fury at the champions of freedom,
Fury at the enthusiasts of the yoke,
Fury at boors and gentlemen—
Specimens of various stripes
Of that same "worldly wisdom"—
At the world and at my native land.

Fury? More likely indifference
To life, eternity, and fate.
Something cat- or bird-like—
It disturbs them,
Those true knights of decency,
Respectable Mr. A and Mr. B,
So comfortably ensconced there.

Туман. Передо мной дорога,
По ней привычно я бреду.
От будущего я немного,
Точнее — ничего не жду.
Не верю в милосердье Бога,
Не верю, что сгорю в аду.

Так арестанты по этапу
Плетутся из тюрьмы в тюрьму . . .
. . . Мне лев протягивает лапу
И я её любезно жму.

— Как поживаете, коллега?
Вы тоже спите без простынь?
Что на земле белее снега,
Прозрачней воздуха пустынь?

Вы убежали из зверинца?
Вы — царь зверей. А я — овца
В печальном положеньи принца
Без королевского дворца.

Без гонорара. Без короны.
Со всякой сволочью «на ты».
Смеются надо мной вороны,
Царапают меня коты.

Mist. The road in front of me,
The one I always wander down.
From the future I expect little,
To be more precise—nothing.
I don't believe in God's mercy,
I don't believe I'll burn in hell.

Thus convicts along transit routes
Trudge from prison to prison . . .
. . . A lion stretches out its paw
And I squeeze it obligingly.

How are you, colleague?
You too sleep without sheets?
What on earth is whiter than snow,
More transparent than the air of deserts?

You escaped from the zoo?
You—the king of beasts. And me—a sheep
In the sad situation of a prince
Without a royal palace.

Without royalties, without a crown,
On familiar terms with all the scum.
Crows laugh at me,
And cats scratch me.

Пускай царапают, смеются,
Я к этому привык давно.
Мне счастье поднеси на блюдце—
Я выброшу его в окно.

Стихи и звёзды остаются
А остальное—всё равно!...

Let them scratch, let them laugh,
I'm long used to all that.
Bring me happiness on a plate—
I'll throw it out the window.

Poems and stars remain
As for the rest—who cares!

Отвлечённой сложностью персидского ковра,
Суетливой роскошью павлиньего хвоста
В небе расцветают и темнеют вечера.
О, совсем бессмысленно и всё же неспроста.

Голубая яблоня над кружевом моста
Под прозрачно призрачной верленовской луной—
Миллионнолетняя земная красота,
Вечная бессмыслица—она опять со мной.

В общем, это правильно, и я ещё дышу.
Подвернулась музыка: её и запишу.
Синей паутиною (хвоста или моста),
Линией павлиньей. И всё же неспроста.

As the abstract complexity of a Persian rug,
As the busy luxury of a peacock's tail
Evenings bloom and darken in the sky.
O, quite ridiculous, yet not in vain.

A sky-blue apple tree above a lacy bridge
Under a transparent spectral Verlaine moon—
The million-year-old earthly beauty,
Eternal absurdity—it's by my side again.

In general, that's right, and I'm still breathing.
Some music came my way: I'll write it down.
As a blue mesh (of a tail, or a bridge),
As a motley peacock line. Yet not in vain.

ПОСМЕРТНЫЙ ДНЕВНИК
POSTHUMOUS DIARY
1958

Александр Сергеич, я о вас скучаю.
С вами посидеть бы, с вами б выпить чаю.
Вы бы говорили, я б, развесив уши,
Слушал бы да слушал.

Вы мне всё роднее, вы мне всё дороже.
Александр Сергеич, вам пришлось ведь тоже
Захлебнуться горем, злиться, презирать,
Вам пришлось ведь тоже трудно умирать.

Aleksandr Sergeich, how much I miss you.
If you and I could sit a while, have some tea together.
You would speak, and I, ears wide,
I would listen and listen.

You grow ever closer, ever dearer to me.
Aleksander Sergeich, you too had to
Choke on woe, to fume, to despise,
And you too came to hard dying.

Кошка крадётся по светлой дорожке,
Много ли горя в кошачьей судьбе?
Думать об этой обмызганной кошке
Или о розах. Забыть о себе.

Вечер июльский томительно душен.
Небо в окне, как персидская шаль.
Даже к тебе я почти равнодушен.
Даже тебя мне почти уж не жаль.

A cat slinks along a bright pathway,
Is there much sorrow in a feline fate?
Think about this mangy cat
Or about these roses. Forget about yourself.

This July evening is suffocatingly sultry.
The sky in the window is like a Persian shawl.
Even to you I'm almost indifferent.
Even for you I already have no pity, almost.

Я жил как будто бы в тумане,
Я жил как будто бы во сне.
В мечтах, в трансцендентальном плане,
И вот пришлось проснуться мне.

Проснуться, чтоб увидеть ужас,
Чудовищность моей судьбы.
. . . О русском снеге, русской стуже . . .
Ах, если б, если б . . . да кабы . . .

I lived as if it were in a fog,
I lived as if it were in a dream,
In fancies, on a transcendental plane—
And now to me it has fallen to wake.

To wake to see the horror,
The hideousness of my fate.
. . . About Russian snow, deep Russian frost . . .
Ah, if only, only . . . go on wishing . . .

Мне уж не придётся впредь
Чистить зубы, щёки брить.
«Перед тем, как умереть
Надо же поговорить».

В вечность распахнулась дверь,
И «пора, мой друг, пора!» . . .
Просветлиться бы теперь,
Жизни прокричать ура!

Стариковски помудреть,
С миром душу примирить . . .
. . . Перед тем, как умереть,
Не о чем мне говорить.

From now on, I won't have the need
To brush my teeth, to shave my cheeks.
"Before one is to die,
One's got to talk a bit."

The door to eternity has opened wide,
And ". . . 'tis time, my friend, 'tis time!"
If I could get enlightened now—
Shout hurrah to life,

Get an old man's wisdom,
Make my soul's peace with the world . . .
. . . Before I am to die,
I've got nothing to talk about.

В громе ваших барабанов
Я сторонкой проходил —
В стадо золотых баранов
Не попал. Не угодил.

А хотелось, не скрываю, —
Слава, деньги и почёт.
В каторге я изнываю,
Чёрным дням ведя подсчёт.

Сколько их ещё до смерти —
Три или четыре дня?
Ну, а всё-таки, поверьте,
Вспомните и вы меня.

I kept my distance
From the thunder of your drums—
I didn't fall in with the flock of golden sheep.
No such luck.

But I did want—I won't hide it—
Fame, money, and honors.
I waste away, sentenced to hard labor,
Keeping track of the black days.

How many more of them until death—
Three or four days?
But all the same, trust me,
Even you will remember me.

А может быть, ещё и не конец?
Терновый мученический венец
Ещё мой не украсит лоб
И в fosse commune мой нищий ящик-гроб
Не сбросят в этом богомерзком Йере.

Могу ж я помечтать, по крайней мере,
Что я ещё лет десять проживу.
Свою страну увижу наяву —
Нева и Волга, Невский и Арбат —
И буду я прославлен и богат,
Своей страны любимейший поэт . . .

Вздор! Ерунда! Ведь я давно отпет.
На что надеяться, о чём мечтать?
Я даже не могу с кровати встать.

But maybe it's not quite the end?
A thorny martyr's wreath
Won't yet beautify my brow,
And my pauper's coffin box will not be
Tossed into a *fosse commune* in godforsaken Hyères.

May I dream a bit, at least,
That I'll live another ten years?
That I'll see my country in the flesh—
The Neva and Volga, the Nevsky and the Arbat—
And I will be famous and rich,
The favorite poet of my country . . .

Rubbish! Nonsense! I'm all sung out long ago.
What's to hope, what's to dream about?
I can't even get out of bed.

Воскресенье. Удушья прилив и отлив,
Стал я как-то не в меру бесстыдно болтлив.

Мне всё хочется что-то своё досказать,
Объяснить, уточнить, разъяснить, доказать.

Мне с читателем хочется поговорить,
Всех, кто мне помогали — поблагодарить.

Есть такие прекрасные люди средь вас.
Им земной мой поклон в предпоследний мой час.

Sunday. The ebb and flow of suffocation;
Somehow I've become shamelessly, overly garrulous.

I keep wanting to finish saying what is mine alone,
To explain, make precise, clarify, prove.

I keep wanting to speak with my reader,
To thank all those who have helped me.

There are such wonderful people among you.
To them I bow low in my penultimate hour.

Ку-ку-реку или бре-ке-ке-ке?
Крыса в груди или жаба в руке?

Можно о розах, можно о пне.
Можно о том, что неможется мне.

Ну, и так далее. И потому,
Ангел мой, зла не желай никому.

Бедный мой ангел, прощай и прости! . .
Дальше с тобою мне не по пути.

Cock-a-doodle-do or ribb-be-et?
A rat in the chest or a toad in the hand?

I can go on about roses, or about a tree stump.
I can go on about my not feeling well.

And so forth, you know. Therefore,
My angel, don't wish anyone ill.

My poor angel, farewell and forgive!
From here you must go on without me.

Аспазия, всегда Аспазия,
Красивая до безобразия —
И ни на грош разнообразия.

А кто она была такая?..
И кто такая Навзикая?..

Себя зевотой развлекая,
Лежу, как зверь больной, в берлоге я —
История и мифология.

А за окошком нудь и муть,
Хотелось бы и мне уснуть.
Нельзя — бессонница терзает.

Вот ёлочка, а вот и белочка,
Из-за сугроба вылезает,
Глядит немного оробелочка,
Орешки продает в кредит
И по ночам прилежно спит.

Aspasia, always Aspasia,
Beautiful, crazy beautiful—
And without an ounce of variety.

And who was she anyway?
And who was this Nausicaa?

Amusing myself with yawning,
I lie in my lair like a sick animal—
History and mythology.

Outside the window boredom and dullness,
I too feel like falling asleep.
Not possible—insomnia torments me.

Here's a little spruce, and here a little squirrel
Crawls out from behind a snowdrift,
Shy squirrelette looks about a bit,
Sells her nut kernels on credit
And sleeps diligently every night.

Ночь, как Сахара, как ад, горяча.
Дымный рассвет. Полыхает свеча.
Вот начертил на блокнотном листке
Я Размахайчика в чёрном венке,
Лапки и хвостика тонкая нить . . .

«В смерти моей никого не винить».

The night is hot, like the Sahara, like hell.
A smoky sunrise. The candle is blazing.
Here I've sketched on a notebook page
Mr. Tailwagger in a black wreath,
The thin thread of his little paw and tail.

"Don't blame anyone for my death."

Ночных часов тяжёлый рой.
Лежу измученный жарой
И снами, что уже не сны.
Из раскалённой тишины
Вдруг раздаётся хрупкий плач.
Кто плачет так? И почему?
Я вглядываюсь в злую тьму
И понимаю не спеша,
Что плачет так моя душа
От жалости и страха.
—Не надо. Нет, не плачь.
. . . О, если бы с размаха
Мне голову палач!

The heavy swarm of night hours.
I lie tormented by the heat
And by dreams that are no longer dreams.
From the blistering hot silence
There suddenly sounds a frail crying.
Who's crying so? And why?
I peer into the evil darkness
And I realize without haste
That it is my soul crying so
From pity and fear.
"Don't. No, don't cry."
O, if only an executioner
Would lop off my head with one swing!

На барабане б мне погреметь—
Само-убийство.

              О, если б посметь!
Если бы сил океанский прилив!
Друга, врага, да и прочих простив.
Без барабана. И вовсе не злой.
Узкою бритвой иль скользкой петлёй.
—Страшно?.. А ты говорил—развлечение.
Видишь, дружок, как меняется мнение.

I would like to beat out on drums—
"Sui-cide."

                    O, if only I had the guts!
If only I had an ocean tide of strength!
—Having forgiven friend, foe, and sundry others.
Without a drum. Not malicious at all.
With a narrow razor or a slippery noose.
Scary? And you said "amusement."
See, dear friend, how opinion changes.

Дымные пятна соседних окон,
Розы под ветром вздыхают и гнутся.
Если б поверить, что жизнь это сон,
Что после смерти нельзя не проснуться.

Будет в раю — рай совсем голубой —
Ждать так прохладно, блаженно-беспечно.
И никогда не расстаться с тобой!
Вечно с тобой. Понимаешь ли? Вечно . . .

Smoky blotches of neighbor windows,
Roses sigh and bend in the wind.
If one could believe that life is a dream,
That one cannot not awake after death.

In paradise—deep-blue paradise—
Waiting will be so fresh and blessedly carefree.
And never to part from you!
Eternally with you. Do you understand? Eternally . . .

Меня уносит океан
То к Петербургу, то к Парижу.
В ушах тимпан, в глазах туман,
Сквозь них я слушаю и вижу —

Сияет соловьями ночь,
И звёзды, как снежинки, тают,
И души — им нельзя помочь —
Со стоном улетают прочь,
Со стоном в вечность улетают.

The ocean carries me off
Now to Petersburg, now to Paris.
A timpani in my ears, mist in my eyes,
Through them I listen and see—

The night glows with nightingales,
And stars melt like snowflakes,
And souls, they are beyond help,
With sobs they fly away,
With sobs they fly into eternity.

Зачем, как шальные, свистят соловьи
Всю южную ночь до рассвета?
Зачем драгоценные плечи твои . . .
Зачем? . . Но не будет ответа.

Не будет ответа на вечный вопрос
О смерти, любви и страданьи,
Но вместо ответа над ворохом роз,
Омытое ливнями звуков и слёз,
                Сияет воспоминанье
О том, чем я вовсе и не дорожил,
Когда на земле я томился. И жил.

Why do the nightingales whistle wildly
All through the southern night until dawn?
Why are your precious shoulders . . .
Why? But no answer will come.

No answer will come to the eternal question
About death, love, and suffering,
But instead of an answer, over a pile of roses,
Washed by downpours of sounds and tears,
       Memory glows
Of that which I did not cherish at all,
When here on earth I languished. And lived.

Все розы увяли. И пальма замёрзла.
По мёртвому саду я тихо иду
И слышу, как в небе по азбуке Морзе
Звезда выкликает звезду,
И мне—а не ей—обещает беду.

All the roses faded. And the palm tree froze.
I walk quietly in the dead garden
And I hear how in the sky, in Morse code,
One star calls out another star,
To me—not it—promising woe.

В зеркале сутулый, тощий,
Складки у бессонных глаз.
Это всё гораздо проще,
Будничнее во сто раз.

Будничнее и беднее —
Зноем опалённый сад,
Дно зеркальное. На дне. И
Никаких путей назад:

Я уже спустился в ад.

In the mirror—bent, emaciated,
Wrinkles around sleepless eyes.
It is all much simpler,
A hundred times more humdrum.

More humdrum and poorer still—
A garden scorched by torrid heat,
A mirror bottom. The lower depths.
And there is no way back:

I've already descended into Hell.

«Побрили Кикапу в последний раз,
Помыли Кикапу в последний раз!
Волос и крови полный таз,
            Да-с».

Не так . . . Забыл . . . Но Кикапу
Меня бессмысленно тревожит,
Он больше ничего не может,
Как умереть. Висит в шкапу —
Не он висит, а мой пиджак —
И всё не то, и всё не так.

Да и при чём бы тут кровавый таз?
«Побрили Кикапу в последний раз . . .»

"They shaved the Kickapoo for the last time,
They washed the Kickapoo for the last time!
A full tub of hair and blood,
                    That's right."

Not quite . . . I've forgotten . . . But the Kickapoo
Senselessly upsets me,
There's nothing more he can do,
But to die. Hanging in the closet—
He's not hanging, it's my jacket—
And all is not right, not like it should be.

And what's a blood-filled tub doing here anyway?
"They shaved the Kickapoo for the last time . . ."

Было всё — и тюрьма и сума,
В обладании полном ума,
В обладании полном таланта.
С распроклятой судьбой эмигранта
Умираю . . .

There has been everything—prison and tramping,
In full possession of one's mind,
In full possession of one's talent.
With the accursed fate of an émigré
I'm dying . . .

Пароходы в море тонут,
Опускаются на дно.
Им в междупланетный омут
Окунуться не дано.

Сухо шелестит омела,
Тянет вечностью с планет . . .
. . . И кому какое дело,
Что меня на свете нет?

Ships drown in the sea,
Sinking to the bottom.
To them it is not given
To plunge into the interplanetary whirlpool.

Mistletoe dryly rustles,
Planets smell of eternity . . .
And whose business is it
If I'm in this world or not?

В ветвях олеандровых трель соловья.
Калитка захлопнулась с жалобным стуком.
Луна закатилась за тучи. А я
Кончаю земное хожденье по мукам,

Хожденье по мукам, что видел во сне—
С изгнаньем, любовью к тебе и грехами.
Но я не забыл, что обещано мне
Воскреснуть. Вернуться в Россию—стихами.

The nightingale's trill in the oleander branches.
The gate swung shut with a plaintive bang.
The moon disappeared behind the clouds. And I
Complete my earthly purgatory—

The purgatory that I saw in a dream,
With exile, love for you, and sins.
But I haven't forgotten that to me it is promised
To rise again. To return to Russia—in my poems.

. . . и Леонид под Фермопилами,
Конечно, умер и за них.

Строка за строкой. Тоска. Облака.
Луна освещает приморские дали.
Бессильно лежит восковая рука
В сиянии лунном, на одеяле.
Удушливый вечер бессмысленно пуст.
Вот так же, в мученьях дойдя до предела
Вот так же, как я, умирающий Пруст
Писал, задыхаясь. Какое мне дело
До Пруста и смерти его? Надоело!
Я знать не хочу ничего, никого!

. . .Московские ёлочки,
Снег. Рождество.
И вечер,—по-русскому,—ласков и тих . . .
«И голубые комсомолочки . . .»
«Должно быть, умер и за них».

. . . and Leonidas at Thermopylae,
Of course, he died for them too.

Line after line. Longing. Clouds.
The moon illuminates distant seashores.
The waxen hand lies listlessly
In the lunar light, on a blanket.
The stifling night is senselessly empty.
Just like me, having suffered to the limit,
Just like me, the dying Proust
Wrote, suffocating. What do I care
About Proust and his death? I've had enough!
I don't want to know anything, or anyone!

. . . Little Moscow spruce trees,
Snow. Christmas.
And a Russian evening, caressing and soft . . .
"And Komsomol girls in blue . . ."
"He must have died for them too."

Из спальни уносят лампу,
Но через пять минут
На тоненькой ножке
Лампа снова тут.

Как луна из тумана,
Так легка и бела,
И маленькая обезьяна
Спускается с потолка.

Серая обезьянка,
Мордочка с кулачок,
На спине шарманка,
На голове колпачок.

Садится и медленно крутит ручку
Старой, скрипучей шарманки своей,
И непонятная песня
Баюкает спящих детей:

«Из холода, снега и льда
Зимой расцветают цветы,
Весной цветы облетают
И дети легко умирают.
И чайки летят туда,
Где вечно цветут кресты
На холмиках детских могилок,
Детей, убежавших в рай . . .»

О, пой ещё, обезьянка!
Шарманка, играй, играй!

The lamp is taken from the bedroom,
But in five minutes
The lamp is here again,
Standing on its lanky leg—

Like the moon from the mist,
So light and white.
And a little monkey
Comes down from the ceiling.

A gray little monkey,
Muzzle the size of a small fist,
A street-organ on her back,
A little cap on her head.

She sits and slowly turns the handle
Of her old squeaky street-organ,
And an incomprehensible song
Lulls the sleeping children:

"Flowers blossom in winter
From cold and snow and ice,
In spring flowers fade
And children die peacefully.
And the seagulls fly there
Where crosses bloom eternally
On the little mounds of children's graves,
Of children who ran away to paradise . . ."

O, sing more, little monkey!
Street-organ, play, play on!

А что такое вдохновенье?
—Так . . . Неожиданно, слегка
Сияющее дуновенье
Божественного ветерка.

Над кипарисом в сонном парке
Взмахнёт крылами Азраил—
И Тютчев пишет без помарки:
«Оратор римский говорил . . .»

And just what is inspiration?
—Well . . . Unexpectedly, a slight
Shining puff of
A divine breeze.

Azrael will spread his wings
Above a cypress in a sleepy park—
And Tiutchev needs no draft to write
"The Roman orator once said . . ."

Вас осуждать бы стал с какой же стати я
За то, что мне не повезло?
Уже давно пора забыть понятия:
Добро и зло.

Меня вы не спасли. По-своему вы правы.
—Какой-то там поэт . . .
Ведь до поэзии, до вечной славы
Вам дела нет.

Why should I stand in judgment over you
Because I had no luck?
It's about time we forgot those concepts:
Good and Evil.

You didn't save me. In your own way, you are right.
Some poet or other . . .
After all, for poetry, for eternal glory
You care nothing.

За столько лет такого маянья
По городам чужой земли
Есть от чего прийти в отчаянье,
И мы в отчаянье пришли.

— В отчаянье, в приют последний,
Как будто мы пришли зимой
С вечерни в церковке соседней,
По снегу русскому, домой.

After so many years of such toiling
Among the towns of a foreign land
There is reason to be overcome with despair,
And we have come to despair.

To despair, our last refuge,
As if we've come in wintertime—
After Vespers in some little church next door,
Through Russian snow—home.

До нелепости смешно —
Так бесславно умереть,
Дать себя с земли стереть,
Как чернильное пятно!

Ну, а всё же след чернил,
Разведённых кровью, —
Как склонялся Азраил
Ночью к изголовью,

О мечтах и о грехах,
Странствиях по мукам —
Обнаружится в стихах
В назиданье внукам.

It is ridiculous to absurdity—
To die so ingloriously,
Letting oneself be wiped from the world,
Like a blot of ink!

But still, the trace of this ink,
Infused with blood—
As Azrael bent down
At night over the head of the bed,

About dreams and sins,
Wanderings through Purgatory—
Will be revealed in poems
For the edification of our descendants.

Отчаянье я превратил в игру —
О чём вздыхать и плакать в самом деле?
Ну, не забавно ли, что я умру
Не позже, чем на будущей неделе?

Умру, — хотя ещё прожить я мог
Лет десять иль, пожалуй, даже двадцать.

Никто не пожалел. И не помог.
И вот приходится смываться.

Август 1958

I've turned despair into a game—
What's to sigh and cry about anyway?
And isn't it amusing, that I'll die
No later than next week?

I'll die,—although I could live on
Ten or perhaps even twenty years.

No one took pity. No one helped, either.
And now it's time to slip away.

August 1958

Для голодных собак понедельник,
А для прочего общества вторник.
И гуляет с метёлкой бездельник,
Называется в вечности дворник.

Если некуда больше податься
И никак не добраться домой,
Так давай же шутить и смеяться,
Понедельничный пёсик ты мой.

Август 1958

For hungry dogs it's Monday,
But for the rest of society—Tuesday.
An idler wanders about with a broom,
In eternity he's called the yard man.

If there's nowhere still to go
And no way to get back home,
Then let's joke and laugh,
My little Monday doggy.

August 1958

Теперь бы чуточку беспечности,
Взглянуть на Павловск из окна.
А рассуждения о вечности . . .
Да и кому она нужна?

Не избежать мне неизбежности,
Но в блеске августовского дня
Мне хочется немножко нежности
От ненавидящих меня.

Now I'd like a bit of being carefree,
To glance at Pavlovsk from the window.
As to discussions about eternity . . .
And who needs it anyway?

Not for me to avoid the unavoidable,
But in the bright shine of an August day
I so want a little tenderness
From those who hate me.

Вечер. Может быть, последний
Пустозвонный вечер мой.
Я давно топчусь в передней —
Мне давно пора домой.

В горле тошнотворный шарик,
Смертный вкус на языке,
Электрический фонарик,
Как звезда, горит в руке.

Как звезда, что мне светила,
Путеводно предала,
Предала и утопила
В Средиземных волнах зла.

Август 1958

Evening. Perhaps my last
Pointless evening.
I've long dawdled in the anteroom—
It's long past time for me to go home.

A nauseating lump in my throat,
The taste of death on the tongue,
A battery flashlight,
Like a star, shines in my hand.

Like a star that lit my path,
It betrayed me along the way,
Betrayed and drowned me
In Mediterranean waves of evil.

August 1958

Вот ёлочка. А вот и белочка,
Из-за сугроба вылезает,
Глядит немного оробелочка,
И ничего не понимает—
Ну абсолютно ничего.

Сверкают свечечки на ёлочке,
Блестят орешки золотые,
И в шубках новеньких с иголочки
Собрались жители лесные
Справлять достойно Рождество:
Лисицы, волки, медвежата,
Куницы, лоси остророгие
И прочие четвероногие.

. . . А белочка ушла куда-то
Ушла куда глаза глядят,
Куда Макар гонял телят,
Откуда нет пути назад,
Откуда нет возврата.

1958

Here's a little spruce. And here a little squirrel
Crawls out from behind a snowdrift,
Shy squirrelette looks about a bit,
And doesn't understand a thing—
Absolutely nothing.

Candlettes glimmer on the little spruce,
Golden nutlettes gleam,
The forest dwellers have gathered
In their new fur coats all spic and span
To celebrate Christmas properly:
Foxes, wolves, bear cubs,
Martens, sharp-horned elk,
And other four-footed creatures.

. . . But the little squirrel went off somewhere,
Went off where her eyes took her,
To the back of beyond,
From where no path leads back,
From where there is no return.

1958

Если б время остановить,
Чтобы день увеличился вдвое,
Перед смертью благословить
Всех живущих и всё живое.

И у тех, кто обидел меня,
Попросить смиренно прощенья,
Чтобы вспыхнуло пламя огня
Милосердия и очищенья.

If time could be stopped
So that the day doubled in size,
To bless before dying
All living creatures and all that is alive.

And to beg forgiveness humbly
Of those who have offended me,
So that burst forth a fiery flame
Of mercy and purification.

Ликование вечной, блаженной весны,
Упоительные соловьиные трели
И магический блеск средиземной луны
Головокружительно мне надоели.

Даже больше того. И совсем я не здесь.
Не на юге, а в северной, царской столице.
Там остался я жить. Настоящий. Я — весь.
Эмигрантская быль мне всего только снится —
И Берлин, и Париж, и постылая Ницца.

. . . Зимный день. Петербург. С Гумилёвым вдвоём,
Вдоль замёрзшей Невы, как по берегу Леты,
Мы спокойно, классически просто идем,
Как попарно когда-то ходили поэты.

The exultation of eternal, blessed spring,
The intoxicating nightingale trills
And the magical shimmer of the Mediterranean moon
Have become head-spinningly boring to me.

Even more than that. I'm simply not here.
Not in the South, but in the northern Tsarist capital.
There I remained to live. The real me. All of me.
My émigré story is only a dream—
Berlin, and Paris, and repellent Nice.

. . . A winter day. Petersburg. Gumilyov and I,
We walk calmly, with classic simplicity,
Along the frozen, Lethe-like Neva,
As poets of old were wont to stroll, in pairs.

Бороться против неизбежности
И злой судьбы мне не дано.
О, если б мне немного нежности
И вид на «Царское» в окно
На солнечную ту аллею,
Ту, по которой ты пришла.
Я даже вспоминать не смею,
Какой прелестной ты была
С большой охапкою сирени,
Вся в белом, в белых башмаках,
Как за тобой струились тени
И ветра ласковый размах
Играл твоими волосами
И теребил твой чёрный бант . . .

—Но объясни, что стало с нами
И отчего я эмигрант?

To me is not given to struggle
Against inevitability and an evil fate.
O, if I had a bit of tenderness
And a view of Tsarskoe in my window,
Of that sunlit pathway,
The one you came along.
I do not even dare recall
How lovely you were
With that large armful of lilacs,
All in white, in white dress shoes.
How shadows flowed behind you
And the wind's caressing sweep
Played with your hair
And fondled your black bow . . .

But tell me, what happened to us
And why am I an exile?

В небе нежно тают облака:
Всё обдумано и всё понятно.
Если б не бессонная тоска,
Здесь бы мне жилось почти приятно
И спокойно очень. Поутру
Вкусно выпить кофе, прогуляться
И, затеяв сам с собой игру,
Средь мимоз и пальм мечтам предаться,
Чувствуя себя — вот здесь — в саду,
Как портрет без сходства в пышной раме . . .

Если бы забыть, что я иду
К смерти семимильными шагами.

Clouds tenderly melt in the sky:
All is thought out and all makes sense.
If only there were no sleepless yearning,
I could live here almost pleasantly
And quite peacefully. Of a morning
Savor a cup of coffee, have a stroll
And, taking up a game with myself,
Give in to dreams among the mimosas and palms,
Feeling, here, in this very garden,
Like a portrait without likeness in an opulent frame . . .

If I could but forget that I am heading
Toward death with giant strides.

Во сне я думаю о разном,
Но больше всё о безобразном,

О том, что лучше промолчать,
Когда вам нечего сказать,

Что помнить следует об этом
Зря разболтавшимся поэтам.

In my sleep I think of various things,
But most of all of the abominable,

Of how it is better to remain silent,
When you've got nothing to say,

Vainly chattering poets
Should keep this in mind.

Поговори со мной ещё немного,
Не засыпай до утренней зари.
Уже кончается моя дорога,
О, говори со мною, говори!

Пускай прелестных звуков столкновенье,
Картавый, лёгкий голос твой
Преобразят стихотворенье
Последнее, написанное мной.

Август 1958

Speak to me yet a little more,
Don't fall asleep before the break of dawn.
My road is now ending,
O, speak to me, do speak!

May the collision of lovely sounds,
Your lilting, light voice
Transfigure a poem,
The last one written by me.

August 1958

NOTES

This bilingual edition of Georgy Ivanov's poems is the first attempt to create a representative corpus of his mature verse in English. The translators and editors of this book have naturally benefited from the scholarship of their predecessors, and we gratefully acknowledge here our indebtedness to the work of the explorers, interpreters, and editors of Ivanov's poetry and poetics—as well as his biography—including Andrei Arieff, Margaret Dalton, Vadim Kreid, Vladimir Markov, Georgy Moseshvili, Vsevolod Setchkarev, and Evgeni Vitkovsky.

Andrei Arieff's annotated Russian edition of Ivanov's poems—Georgii Ivanov, *Stikhotrovreniia* (Sankt-Peterburg: Akademicheskii Proekt, 2005)—served as the source for all of our choices in the area of orthography, spelling, and punctuation. Arieff's painstaking explication of Ivanov's peculiar brand of lyricism and his voluminous notes accompanying each poem became, in a number of instances, a point of departure (and source of information) for our annotations, and where it was absolutely unavoidable, our explanatory interpretations found below. In assembling these notes, we first and foremost sought to address the needs of a contemporary English-speaking lover of poetry. Thus, no knowledge of Russian language or the literary and/or cultural context of Ivanov's poetry is expected of the reader, although there is no denying that such a knowledge would be of immense benefit for an advanced appreciation of Ivanov the poet. The notes following, therefore, are here to provide our readers with only a sparse set of the most essential, initial bearings; those readers who wish to explore the subject in greater detail are invited to turn to our Russian sources, starting perhaps with the original Russian texts reproduced here alongside our English renderings.

The translators and editors of the present volume are united in their acknowledgment of the fact that no foreign-language paraphrase can ever be turned into an ideal substitute for the original. One's realization of this stark and hardly original truth, however, must not be permitted to arrest permanently one's fulfillment of a moral and ethical imperative that is—or, it seems to us, should be—a main driving force behind every venture into literary translation. One cannot hope to create an ideal translation. One is obliged to transform one's certitude of the importance and value of a given foreign poetic utterance into an attempt to carry this notion across linguistic divides with the aid of all the means at one's disposal. Translations, of course, have a demonstrable potential to replace the originals in the eyes of their readers, unable as those readers often are to compare a text written in a language known to them with the original they have little or no means of understanding. Stripping Ivanov's poems of many such quintessential, seemingly inalienable Russian attributes as meter, rhyme, and alliteration, we sought to gain enough linguistic freedom to compose English versions that at no point obscure the originals. Even more importantly, we attempted to prevent our translations from misplacing what for the Russian poems collected here was their initial orientation toward those universal human experiences that called them into being. The reader may judge how successful we have been in our undertaking.

We are most grateful to Viggo Mortensen and Perceval Press for all their support, patience, and unfailing faith in this project—without that backing and encouragement, we would not have been able to bring this ambitious enterprise to its conclusion.

ROSES

The collection *Roses* first appeared in print in Paris in early 1931. Published by an émigré publishing house called Rodnik/La Source, it quickly became an event in the literary life of the Russian diaspora. Numerous critics greeted *Roses* not only as Ivanov's first truly original work, but they also sensed in it an outstandingly effective expression of the existential predicament of Russian expatriates scattered around the world in the aftermath of the calamitous events of 1917 and the Civil War that followed. *Roses* proved to be a watershed in the author's literary career, revealing him as a leading poetic voice of his generation. Even though—for reasons that had nothing to do with art—Ivanov's poetry did not reach the overwhelming majority of Russian readers in his homeland until the mid-1980s, it is the Ivanov of *Roses* and his subsequent poetic output that place him in the front ranks of modern Russian poets.

Над закатами и розами / Above sunsets and roses (pp. 24–25)
> First published in 1930 in the prominent Parisian émigré periodical *Sovremennye zapiski* (Contemporary Annals).

Глядя на огонь или дремля / Peering at the fire or drowsing (pp. 26–27)
> First published in 1927 and dated "January 1927."

Синий вечер, тихий ветер / Blue evening, soft wind (pp. 28–29)
> First published in an émigré literary collection entitled *Chisla* ([Book of] Numbers).

Душа черства. И с каждым днём черствей / My soul is coarse, and coarser with each day (pp. 30–31)
> First published 1925 and reprinted in 1928. Arieff aptly underscores the fact that this poem is rich in literary allusions, specifically those referring to Don Juan's final lines in Aleksandr Pushkin's "little tragedy" *Kamennyi gost'* (*The Stone Guest*, 1826–30); in these lines Don Juan accepts a fatal handshake from the cemetery monument to a man—the Commendatore of the Mozart opera—wronged and murdered by the notorious libertine. This reference, in its turn, leads to Aleksandr Blok's exploration of the Don Juan theme in his poem "Shagi komandora" ("The Steps of the Commander," 1910). The opening phrase of Ivanov's poem brings to mind *"Dusha moia mrachna. Skorei, pevets, skorei!"* (*"Evreiskaia melodiia"* [Iz Bairona], 1836), Mikhail Lermontov's rendition of Byron's "My soul is dark— Oh! quickly string" (*Hebrew Melodies*, 1815); a direct evocation of the poet whom Russians long held to be the preeminent representative of English Romanticism follows shortly (see "Like Byron to Greece, O, without regret" below).

Не было измены. Только тишина / There was no betrayal. Only silence (pp. 32–33)

First published in 1927 in *Sovremennye zapiski*. The poem was set to music and made into a "romance" by singer, songwriter, and performer Aleksandr Vertinskii (1889–1957).

Напрасно пролита кровь / Blood is spilled in vain (pp. 34–35)

First published in 1926.

Перед тем, как умереть / Before one is to die (pp. 36–37)

First published in *Chisla* in 1930. Arieff suggests that in more than one way the poem constitutes a response to the publication of *The Trout Breaks the Ice* (1929), the last verse collection by Mikhail Kuzmin (1872–1936), who was a leading Russian post-Symbolist poet and a major beacon of Ivanov's poetic apprenticeship.

Я слышу — история и человечество / I hear: "history and mankind (pp. 38–39)

First published in *Sovremennye zapiski* in 1930.

Тёплый ветер веет с юга / A warm wind wafts from the south (pp. 40–41)

First published in *Sovremennye zapiski* in 1930. In this poem Arieff detects a deliberate echoing of poems by Ivanov's older contemporary Aleksandr Blok and his friend Osip Mandelstam.

Балтийское море дымилось / The Baltic Sea was smoking (pp. 42–43)

First published in 1924. Kronstadt is a fortified island and a Russian Baltic Fleet naval base in the Gulf of Finland; Kronstadt has guarded approaches to Petersburg-Petrograd since its founding in 1704 by Peter I. During the Bolshevik coup d'état of 1917 (the so-called October Revolution), sailors from Kronstadt participated in the overthrow of the Kerensky regime, later joining with the Bolsheviks during the Civil War, only to revolt against them in 1921. The Kronstadt rebellion was brutally suppressed by the Bolsheviks, and many people believed that Nikolai Gumilyov (1886–1921)—Ivanov's *maître* and leader of the Acmeist movement in Russian poetry—was executed by the Bolsheviks for his connection to the mutineers.

Чёрная кровь из открытых жил / Black blood from opened veins (pp. 44–45)

First published in 1928.

Как в Грецию Байрон, о, без сожаленья / Like Byron to Greece, O, without regret (pp. 46–47)

First published in 1921. Lord George Gordon Noel Byron (1788–1824) died attempting to help the Greeks in their War of Independence against the Ottoman Empire. The poem alludes to the Russian variant of the famous Latin saying "*per aspera ad astra.*" Its Russian variant can be translated as "through thorns, toward stars" ("*cherez ternii k zvezdam*"; compare Ivanov's "*. . . through stars . . . through midnight and roses . . .*").

Это только синий ладан / This is only blue incense (pp. 48–49)

Ivanov reproduced this poem (without the last stanza) in *Embarkation to the Island of Cythera* in 1937.

В сумраке счастья неверного / In the twilight of unfaithful happiness (pp. 50–51)

First published in *Sovremennye zapiski* in 1930.

Увяданьем еле тронут / Barely touched by decay (pp. 54–55)
First published in the prominent Paris-based émigré daily *Poslednie novosti* (Latest News) in 1930.

Прислушайся к дальнему пенью / Give ear to the distant singing (pp. 56–57)
First published in 1926. "Aeolian harp" is sometimes also identified as a lyre. Ivanov may have in mind Samuel Taylor Coleridge's "The Aeolian Harp," a signal poem for the Romantic movement.

Когда-нибудь и где-нибудь / Sometime and somewhere (pp. 60–61)
First published in *Poslednie novosti* in 1928.

Злой и грустной полоской рассвета / Like a bitter, sad streak of daybreak (pp. 62–63)
First published in *Poslednie novosti* in 1928.

Закроешь глаза на мгновенье / Close your eyes for a moment (pp. 64–65)
First published in 1925.

Хорошо, что нет Царя / Nice—there is no Tsar (pp. 66–67)
First published in 1930 in *Chisla*.

В тринадцатом году, ещё не понимая / In 1913, not understanding yet (pp. 68–69)
First published in 1926. In many ways, 1913—the year of the tercentenary of the Romanov dynasty—became the apogee of the Russian Empire; it was, however, soon to be brought down in the wake of the World War I and the revolutions and civil unrest that followed.

Россия, Россия «рабоче-крестьянская» / Russia, the Russia of "workers and peasants" (pp. 70–71)
First published in *Sovremennye zapiski* in 1930.

Холодно бродить по свету / How cold it is to roam the world (pp. 72–73)
First published in *Sovremennye zapiski* in 1930. Donna Anna is a heroine of a number of sources built around the image of Don Juan, of which Mozart's opera *Don Giovanni* (1787) is but one important representative. Ivanov's poem indirectly echoes the eponymous heroine of Pushkin's *Kamennyi gost'* and directly cites Blok's "Shagi komandora" (see above).

По улицам рассеянно мы бродим / Absent-minded, we wander the streets (pp. 74–75)
The first-person plural pronoun of this poem designates the uprooted tribe of Russian émigré intellectuals in Paris, a city that by the early 1930s had become the de facto "capital" of the anti-Bolshevik Russian diaspora. To the new generation of Russian writers and poets outside of Russia—those for whom their homeland was but a memory—Ivanov and his on-and-off friend, the critic and poet Georgy Adamovich (1894–1972), symbolized a living link with a fabulous era of pre-Revolutionary St. Petersburg with its autumnal blossoming of the arts, culture, and literature. Supporting themselves by working a wide array of transient day jobs, these young people flocked in the evenings to such gathering spots as the Monmartre cafés La Bolée, La Coupole, Café du Dôme, Napoli, and Sélect where, under the guidance of their acknowledged *maîtres* Ivanov and Adamovich, they attempted to develop a special "Parisian school" of Russian poetry. United by their

search for "true words" and a mutual rejection of the means of artistic expression they had come to see as "imprecise," these younger followers of Adamovich and Ivanov sought to find expression for their sense of displacement and disconnection and attempted to come to terms with the loss of their homeland. Apart from such genuine (and belatedly recognized) talents as the poets Yuri Mandelstam (1908–1943, no relation to Osip), Boris Poplavsky (1903–1935), Anatoly Steiger (1907–1944), Yuri Terapiano (1892–1980), and others, there appeared on the fringes of this circle such personages as Paul Gorguloff (also known as Pavel Gorgulov, 1895–1932), a Russian proto-Nazi with literary pretentions who, on May 7, 1932, assassinated French President Paul Doumer (see Ivanov's sarcastic—and unwittingly prophetic—reference to an imaginary act of terror against such an important French cultural institute as the Paris Grand Opéra).

Для чего, как на двери небесного рая / Why, as at the gates of heavenly paradise (pp. 76–77)
> First published in 1926.

Страсть? А если нет и страсти / Passion? What if there isn't any passion (pp. 78–79)
> Published previously in 1930.

Как грустно и всё же как хочется жить / How sad—and still one so wants to live (pp. 80–81)
> Place de la Concorde: The largest and most well-known public square in Paris, it lies between the Jardin des Tuileries and the Champs-Élysées. At the time of the French Revolution the area was known as "Place de la Révolution," and (among many others), Marie Antoinette was guillotined there in 1793, as was the revolutionary leader Maximilien Robespierre in 1794. For Ivanov and his contemporary émigré readers, the sparkling lights of the Place de la Concorde embodied their alienation from the prosperity and well-being of their foreign surroundings.

Так тихо гаснул этот день. Едва / This day faded so quietly. The burnished (pp. 82–83)
> First published in 1928.

Грустно, друг. Всё слаще, всё нежнее / It is sad, my friend. The sea breeze ever (pp. 84–85)
> First published in 1926. Ivanov's references to Scotland should be viewed against the backdrop of that country's close identification with Romanticism (James Macpherson's *Ossian* in the 1760s perhaps may be considered the springboard text for European and American Romanticism). Robert Burns's *Poems, Chiefly in the Scottish Dialect* (1786) and Sir Walter Scott's historical *Waverly* novels (from 1814) helped to define and extend the Romantic manifesto of Wordsworth's *Preface* to *Lyrical Ballads* (1800). This reference to Scotland is also an indirect allusion to Mikhail Iur'evich Lermontov (1814–1841), a poet and novelist central to Russia's own Romantic tradition. Excited by a family tradition that credited a Scotsman named George Learmonth with establishing his aristocratic line in Russia, Lermontov made his personal connection to Scotland a key part of his Romantic legend, as can be seen in his poems such as "Ballada" ("A Ballad," 1830) and "Mogila Ossiana" ("The Tomb of Ossian," 1830). This evocation of

Scotland and Lermontov provides Ivanov with an opportunity to enrich his poem with allusions to both English and Russian Romantic traditions and orient his own poetry toward them.

Не спится мне. Зажечь свечу / I can't sleep. Light a candle (pp. 86–87)
First published in 1928.

Как лёд наше бедное счастье растает / Our meager happiness melts like ice (pp. 88–89)
First published in 1926.

Январский день. На берегу Невы / January day, at the Neva's shore (pp. 90–91)
First published in 1928. Teeming with references to the giddy artistic and Bohemian atmosphere of pre-Revolutionary St. Petersburg, this poem is not only a nostalgic farewell to Ivanov's youth, but also a successful attempt on the author's part to underscore the lineage of his lyricism and showcase its roots in the literary tradition of Russia's cultural capital. Ivanov demonstrates himself to be a living link to an era that at the time of this poem's composition and publication already appeared to his younger Russian émigré contemporaries in Paris to be both mythic and unattainable. Each of the ensuing proper names and toponyms is full of implied references to the notable participants and events of that fecund era. Actress and artist Olechka Sudeikina (Olga Afanas'evna Glebova-Sudeikina, 1885–1945) was a frequenter of the literary/artistic cabaret called the Stray Dog (Brodiachaia sobaka, 1912–15) and a model for numerous poets and artists. In her youth, the great poet Anna Akhmatova (pseudonym of Anna Andreevna Gorenko, 1889–1966) was another notable participant in the Stray Dog circle; tall and elegant, she too became a muse to poets and artists (of the latter, most notably Amedeo Modigliani). One of Akhmatova's most enduring accomplishments was to be her *Requiem* (1935–1940), a heart-wrenching narrative poem written from the point of view of a victim of Stalinist terror. An author of a book of poetry, Pallada (Pallada Olimpovna Starynkevich, 1887–1968) earned her place in the Stray Dog legend primarily through her attractiveness (and promiscuity). Renowned for her beauty, Salomea (Salomeia Nikolaevna [Ivanovna] Andronikova-Gal'pern, 1888–1982) was another member of this illustrious circle and a woman of whom Osip Mandelstam was once enamored (Mandelstam's poem "Solominka" ["The Little Straw," 1916] is addressed to her). Pavlovsk: an imperial family residence and magnificent park about twenty miles south of St. Petersburg. In his autobiographical memoir *Shum vremeni* (*The Noise of Time*, 1923), Mandelstam vividly depicts Pavlovsk as a musical and cultural center in the 1890s. Tsarskoe: established in 1710 just a few miles from Pavlovsk, Tsarskoe Selo consists of a chain of parks, including that adjacent to the palace of Catherine the Great. A cultural, tourist, and scientific center, it contained the famous Imperial Lycée from which Russia's greatest poet, Aleksandr Pushkin, and other notables graduated (in a crude, misguided attempt to honor the great poet's memory, the Soviets renamed Tsarskoe Selo "Pushkin"). Vsevolod Kniazev (1891–1913) was an aspiring poet, military officer, and former lover of the famous openly gay

Petersburg poet, composer, diarist, and prose writer Mikhail Kuzmin (1872–1936). Kniazev left Kuzmin, having fallen in love with Olga Sudeikina (see above), then wife of the artist Sergei Sudeikin, but his love was unrequited and he committed suicide in 1913.

Синеватое облако / A bluish cloud (pp. 92–93)

First published in 1927 in *Sovremennye zapiski*.

В глубине, на самом дне сознанья / In the depths, at the very bottom of consciousness (pp. 94–95)

First published in 1929 in *Poslendnie novosti*.

Утро было как утро. Нам было довольно приятно / A morning like any other. We were quite content (pp. 96–97)

First published in 1930 in *Chisla*. As Arieff points out, the "mumbling Englishmen" of the poem are awkwardly attempting to express their appreciation for the ordeals suffered by Ivanov's now nonexistent homeland that—when still named "Russia" and not the "Soviet Union"—was England's World War I ally; its loss was lamented by, among others, Rudyard Kipling (see his "Russia to the Pacifists," 1918).

Медленно и неуверенно / Slowly and timidly (pp. 98–99)

First published in 1928 in *Poslendnie novosti*. "Pushkin mortgaged his estate / [o]r was jealous of his wife"—the reference is of course to Aleksandr Sergeevich Pushkin (1799–1837), Russia's national poet. Pushkin's marriage to Natalia Nikolaevna Goncharova (1812–1863) did not become an enduring source of domestic bliss for him. Having inspired some of Pushkin's most sublime love lyrics, the poet's courtship of and subsequent marriage to Goncharova also forced him to face the reality of providing for a large and growing family. Worst of all, as husband of a stunningly beautiful young woman, Pushkin had to deal with constant encroachments on his private life orchestrated by his high-society enemies. An alleged spousal infidelity and a carefully orchestrated slander campaign centered around it eventually led to Pushkin's death in a duel to which he had challenged a dashing and vacuous army officer, an exiled French legitimist in Russian military service.

От синих звёзд, которым дела нет / From blue stars, who are indifferent to (pp. 100–01)

First published in 1925.

Даль грустна, ясна, холодна, темна / The melancholy distance, clear, cold, and dark (pp. 102–03)

First published in 1927.

Все розы, которые в мире цвели / All the roses that bloomed in the world (pp. 104–05)

First published in 1929 in *Poslednie novosti*.

from EMBARKATION FOR THE ISLAND OF CYTHERA

The title of this collection of Ivanov's poems, which was published in early 1937, replicated that of his debut book of poetry, *Embarkation for I. Cythera* (1911). As follows from the subtitle of the book ("Selected Poems 1916–1936"), it was to represent the evolution of Ivanov's poetry over an entire period of his life and work. The book opened with a section of new, previously uncollected poems (reproduced and translated here), followed by a section of selected poems from *Roses* (1931); the book closed with poems from *Gardens* (1921) and *Heather* (1916).

Kythira—or Cythera—an island off the shore of southern Greece, is at the crossroads of many nations and cultures. In Greek mythology (and subsequently in the neoclassical tradition), the island was believed to have held a Temple of Love and became a destination of Romantic pilgrimage. Having used it twice as a title for his books of poetry, Ivanov clearly nourished a special attachment to this motif, largely because it held a special place in his personal mythology: Ivanov claimed that in his paternal home there was a room decorated with reproductions of an eponymous work by the French artist Antoine Watteau (1684–1721). Watteau's Rococo painting *L'Embarquement pour l'île de Cythère* (*Embarkation for the Island of Cythera*, 1717) was indeed very popular throughout Europe, and it gained the painter entrance to the Académie Royale de Peinture et de Sculpture in Paris. With its flying cupids and all manner of embracing couples, the work supports the legend that Venus emerged from the sea at the island of Cythera.

О, высок, весна, высок твой синий терем / O, spring, high, high your castle blue (pp. 108–09)
> First published in 1931 in *Sovremennye zapiski*. "A ball of yarn rolls on": in Russian fairy tales a ball of yarn capable of showing its owner his/her way is a common attribute of a hero on a quest.

Это месяц плывёт по эфиру / The moon swims in the ether (pp. 110–11)
> First published in 1931 in *Sovremennye zapiski*.

Россия счастие. Россия свет / Russia is happiness. Russia is light (pp. 112–13)
> First published in 1931 in *Sovremennye zapiski*. One of Ivanov's most well-known poetic utterances, to many contemporary Russian readers this is his "signature" poem.

Только всего — простодушный напев / Just that—a simple-hearted melody (pp. 114–15)
> First published in 1931 in *Sovremennye zapiski*.

Слово за словом, строка за строкой / Word after word, line after line (pp. 116–17)
> First published in 1931 in *Sovremennye zapiski*.

Музыка мне больше не нужна / Music is no longer needed by me (pp. 118–19)
> First published in 1931 in *Sovremennye zapiski*.

Звёзды синеют. Деревья качаются / Stars shine deep blue. Trees sway (pp. 120–21)
> First published in 1934 in *Sovremennye zapiski*.

Ни светлым именем богов / Neither by the hallowed name of the gods (pp. 122–23)
>First published in 1931 in *Sovremennye zapiski*.

Только звёзды. Только синий воздух / Only stars, only blue air (pp. 124–25)
>First published in 1931 in *Sovremennye zapiski*.

Сиянье. В двенадцать часов по ночам / The radiance. At midnight every night (pp. 126–27)
>First published in 1932 in *Sovremennye zapiski*. The motif of the dead coming to life at midnight is a reference to the poem "Die nächtliche Heerschau" (1827) by Joseph Christian Freiherr von Zedlitz (Austrian, 1790–1862). Zedlitz's poem was made famous in Russia first by Vasily Zhukovsky, whose inspired translation of it was praised by Pushkin and appeared in print in 1836; the same poem was subsequently adapted by Mikhail Lermontov (1840). The original German poem and its Russian versions alike tell the story of the ghost of Napoleon summoning his lost legions.

Замело тебя, счастье, снегами / Happiness, the snows have covered you (pp. 128–29)
>First published in 1932 in *Sovremennye zapiski*.

О, душа моя, могло ли быть иначе / O, my soul, could it have been different (pp. 130–31)
>First published in 1932 in *Sovremennye zapiski*.

Так иль этак. Так иль этак / This way or that, this way or that (pp. 132–33)
>First published in 1934 in *Sovremennye zapiski*.

Только тёмная роза качнётся / Only the dark rose will sway (pp. 134–35)
>First published in 1931 in *Sovremennye zapiski*.

Я тебя не вспоминаю / I don't care to remember you (pp. 136–37)
>First published in 1936 in *Sovremennye zapiski*.

Над розовым морем вставала луна / The moon came up over the rosy sea (pp. 138–39)
>First published in 1925. The poem was set to music by Aleksandr Vertinsky.

Это звон бубенцов издалёка / It's the sound of yoke-bells from afar (pp. 140–41)
>First published in 1930–31. "It's the sound of yoke-bells from afar"—a lightly paraphrased quotation from a "romance" by poet Aleksandr Kusikov called "Bubentsy"/"Yoke-Bells" (1918), music by Vladimir Bakaleynikov.

В шуме ветра, в детском плаче / In the sound of the wind, in a child's cry (pp. 142–43)
>First published in 1936 in *Sovremennye zapiski*.

Душа человека. Такою / The soul of a man. Never (pp. 144–45)
>First published in 1933.

Жизнь бессмысленную прожил / He lived a senseless life (pp. 146–47)
>First published in 1934.

A PORTRAIT WITHOUT LIKENESS

This collection was issued in 1950 by the Parisian émigré publishing house Rifma ("rhyme" in Russian). It is dedicated to Irina Vladimirovna Odoevtseva (Iraida Gustavovna Geinike, or Iraīda Heinike [Latvian, 1895–1990]), Ivanov's wife and muse. A poet, novelist, and popular—if not altogether reliable—memoirist, Odoevtseva outlived Ivanov; she remarried and later died in Leningrad, USSR. Odoevtseva's return to the USSR in 1987 was seen by many as a remarkable event signifying a reunification of the two branches of Russian literature and culture long separated by civil war and exile.

Что-то сбудется, что-то не сбудется / Something will come true, something not (pp. 150–51)

> The poem was first published in 1949 in *Novyi zhurnal* (*The New Review*), a U.S.–based publishing venture that effectively became a successor to the Russian tradition of the "thick journal" and the diaspora's most illustrious émigré literary magazine *Contemporary Annals* (see above), to which Ivanov frequently contributed during the pre–WWII period of his life and work.

Всё неизменно, и всё изменилось / All is immutable, yet all has changed (pp. 152–53)

> First published in 1947.

Друг друга отражают зеркала / Mirrors reflect each other (pp. 154–55)

> First published in 1950.

Маятника мерное качанье / The measured swing of the pendulum (pp. 156–57)

> First published in 1947. "If only the frost spared the flowers!" is a line borrowed from a simple-hearted folk lament (or rather, a popular literary imitation of a folk song by Count Aleksey Konstantinovich Tolstoy [1817–1875]). It encapsulated Ivanov's less-than-ecstatic retrospective evaluation of his *Roses*, considered by many the quintessence of his lyricism.

Где прошлогодний снег, скажите мне / Where are the snows of yesteryear, tell me (pp. 158–59)

> François Villon (1431–1463): fifteenth-century French poet, vagabond, robber, and brawler known for his 2,000-plus line poem *Grand Testament,* which embeds autobiographical tales in an epic narrative. Highly educated (he held a master's degree), Villon killed a drinking companion in a tavern brawl in 1455 and thereafter did not have a way of making a legitimate living; he had previously been a professor at the Collège de Navarre. He is responsible for the famous phrase "Where are the snows of yesteryear?" ("Mais ou sont les neiges d'antan?"), as translated by the Pre-Raphaelite poet Dante Gabriel Rossetti (1828–1882).

Воскресают мертвецы / The dead are resurrected (pp. 160–61)

> First published in *Novyi zhurnal* in 1949.

Мёртвый проснётся в могиле / A corpse will awaken in his grave (pp. 162–63)

> Volhynia is a region in northwest Ukraine. During World War II the area was the scene of widespread Ukrainian partisan activity and bloody attacks against Polish civilians. Volhynia includes, in part, the swamp-like area of Pripiat Marsh where

major battles of World War I took place. The region was once part of the Polish-Lithuanian kingdom and was incorporated into Soviet Russia after World War II.

Он спал, и Офелия снилась ему / He slept, and dreamed of Ophelia (pp. 164–65)

First published in 1946. Ophelia, a key character in *Hamlet*, is in love with Prince Hamlet, who repays her with cruel rejection. He tells her he did not love her (some critics see deflected rage at his mother Gertrude in Hamlet's behavior towards Ophelia), commanding "Get thee to a nunnery!" (III, i, 124). The loss of her father (the royal counselor Polonius), the absence of her brother Laertes, and Hamlet's rejection lead to Ophelia's watery suicide.

День превратился в своё отраженье / The day has turned into its reflection (pp. 166–67)

First published in 1950.

А люди? Ну на что мне люди / And people? So why do I need people (pp. 170–71)

First published in 1947.

Образ полусотворённый / An image half-created (pp. 172–73)

First published in 1947.

В награду за мои грехи / As reward for my sins (pp. 174–75)

First published in 1950.

Холодно. В сумерках этой страны / Cold. In the twilight of this country (pp. 180–81)

First published in 1947.

Тихим вечером в тихом саду / One quiet evening in a quiet garden (pp. 182–83)

First published in 1947. "An angel carried a star into infinity": this line echoes the central image from a poem by Lermontov ("Angel"/"The Angel," 1831) which describes the torments of a celestial soul condemned to confinement in a mortal body while not being able to forget the heavenly songs it once heard. This reference has another level, as Ivanov's poem harkens back to *"Svirel' zapela na mostu"* ("A pan flute burst into song on a bridge," 1908), a poem by Blok.

Был замысел странно-порочен / The design was strangely flawed (pp. 186–87)

First published in *Sovremennye zapiski* in 1930.

Потеряв даже в прошлое веру / Losing even faith in the past (pp. 188–89)

Cythera, Watteau: in this poem Ivanov returns to the central images of his collection *Embarkation for the Island of Cythera*.

Отражая волны голубого света / Reflecting the waves of the sky-blue light (pp. 190–91)

A reference to Nice, the well-known tourist city in southern France on the Mediterranean, which had been home to Russian sojourners beginning in the nineteenth century, including Chekhov, who lived for seven months at the Pension Russe in Nice in the late 1890s. By 1912 the Russian community had grown so large that Nicholas II had a church constructed there. After the Russian Revolution in 1917, Nice and the surrounding Côte d'Azur became a favorite retreat for Russian émigré writers and artists; Ivan Bunin was a famous neighbor in nearby Grasse.

Ничего не вернуть. И зачем возвращать / You can return nothing. And why bother (pp. 192–93)

First published in 1949.

На грани таянья и льда / On the border of melt and ice (pp. 194–95)

The image of a "greenish star" is, once again, evocative of Blok.

Отвратительнейший шум на свете / The most revolting noise in the world (pp. 196–97)

The poem is based on an actual event: Ivanov's and Odoevtseva's villa was destroyed in an Allied bombing in 1944.

Как туман на рассвете — чужая душа / The soul of another is like a mist at dawn (pp. 198–99)

First published in 1947.

Поговори со мной о пустяках / Speak to me of trifles (pp. 200–01)

The poem is addressed to Odoevtseva.

Лунатик в пустоту глядит / A sleepwalker looks into emptiness (pp. 202–03)

First published in 1949 in *Novyi zhurnal*.

Летний вечер прозрачный и грузный / This summer evening is transparent and bloated (pp. 204–05)

The Itinerants (derived from the Russian word *"peredvizhniki"*) were part of an art movement (1870–1923) begun in the second half of the nineteenth century as a revolt against academic painting. Involving a turn to "ideological realism," the movement had a strong populist tinge. One of its representatives, Ilya Repin, whose work *Volga Barge Haulers* (1870–73; see below) can be taken as emblematic of the group, is still considered one of Russia's outstanding artists.

Теперь тебя не уничтожат / They won't destroy you now (pp. 208–09)

First published in 1949. "[T]hat insane leader" is Hitler, whereas "the Sickle" and "the Eagle" symbolize the two alternative lines of social and political development—as a Communist state or a nationalist Russian empire—envisaged by some of Ivanov's contemporaries as the country's future.

С бесчеловечною судьбой / With this inhuman fate (pp. 216–17)

First published in 1947.

Если бы жить . . . Только бы жить / If I could live, only live (pp. 218–19)

". . . a barge hauler on the Great River . . .": see above for more information about a celebrated painting by Ilya Repin featuring Volga barge haulers. "Let's pull now, heave" is a refrain from a barge hauler's song.

В дыму, в огне, в сияньи, в кружевах / Amid smoke, fire, radiance, and lace (pp. 220–21)

First published in 1926.

Восточные поэты пели / The Oriental poets sang (pp. 222–23)

Omar Khayyám (1048–1131 AD) was a Persian poet known in the West for his narrative poem of love and philosophy, *The Rubáiyát*, rendered famously into subtle, rhymed English by Edward FitzGerald in1859.

Остановиться на мгновенье / To stop for a moment (pp. 224–25)

    The poem's opening line echoes a celebrated Goethean apostrophe, *"Beautiful moment, do not pass away!" ("Verweile doch! du bist so schön!)"* from *Faust*.

У входа в бойни, сквозь стальной туман / Scraping, the crane crawled through (pp. 226–27)

    First published in 1926. The cityscape depicted in the first quatrain invokes that of the St. Petersburg of Ivanov's youth, now vividly remembered by an older, far less exalted poet.

То, о чём искусство лжёт / That about which art tells lies (pp. 228–29)

    "[L]*iving water*": in Russian fairy tales "living water" is endowed with magical properties that bring the dead back to life.

Rayon de rayonne (pp. 232–33)

    Ivanov expounded the meaning of this title as a deliberate hoax, an attempt at re-creating the effect of the nonsensical titles of the Futurist era.

1. В тишине вздохнула жаба / 1. In the quiet a toad sighed (pp. 232–33)

    First published in *Novyi zhurnal* in 1949.

2. Портной обновочку утюжит / 2. The tailor irons a new order (pp. 234–35)

    The poem contains an echo of a poem by Ivanov's literary rival Vladislav Khodasevich: *"Ni zhit', ni pet' pochti ne stoit . . ."* ("There is almost no point in either living or singing," 1922).

3. Всё чаще эти объявления / 3. These announcements come more often (pp. 236–37)

    "Today it's your turn, tomorrow mine!": here Ivanov cites Hermann's aria from Tchaikovsky's *The Queen of Spades*, which premiered in 1890 with a libretto by Modest Tchaikovsky, the composer's brother. *"Ice March"* (1918) refers to a heroic episode by the Russian White Guards in the anti-Bolshevik campaign: a White Army detachment retreated across the frozen steppe from Rostov to Kuban in face of the Red Army pressing down from their north. *"No Captain Ivanóv"*—the position of the stress in this name is a meaningful detail: thus stressed ("ivanOv"), it designates any ordinary man, a "Johnson." It bears repeating that Georgy Ivanov stressed his family name on the first syllable, signifying a more aristocratic descent.

4. Где-то белые медведи / 4. Somewhere white bears (pp. 238–39)

    In keeping with the promise contained in the deliberately nonsensical title of this suite of poems, this piece presents an entire bestiary of creatures seemingly at home in a fairy tale. Arieff points out that the "six-horse carriage" that "won't be bringing anything to me" hints at a reversal of a Cinderella motif peculiar to Ivanov's vision of his lot in life.

5. По улице уносит стружки / 5. An icy November wind (pp. 240–41)

    The epigraph comes from *Corion*, a play by Denis Fonvizin (Russian, 1744–1792). In *Corion* (adapted from the French and premiered in 1764), this remark is made by a peasant (hence the exaggerated country accent) commenting on the state of mind of an aristocratic young lady. *"How boring to live in this world, / [h]ow uncomfortable, ladies and gentlemen!"*: here Ivanov paraphrases the concluding observation made by the narrator in "The Tale of How Ivan Ivanovich Quarreled with Ivan Nikiforovich," a novella by Nikolai Gogol (1809–1852). The protagonist of Ivanov's poem is a Russian émigré living in Europe, where his concerns, both quotidian and philosophical (however shallow and grotesque the latter one may be), remain essentially the same as those portrayed by Gogol in his satirical sketches from the life of nineteenth-century provincial Russian gentry.

6. Зазеваешься, мечтая / 6. Daydreaming, you begin to drift off (pp. 243–44)
First published in 1949. "[L]ittle golden fish": in a famous adaptation of a Russian folk fairy tale by Pushkin, a little golden fish comes to symbolize a chance for luck, wealth, and happiness squandered by stupid and greedy people.

9. В пышном доме графа Зубова / 9. In Count Zuboff's splendid house (pp. 248–49)
First published in 1950. In pre-Revolutionary Petersburg, Count Valentin Platonovich Zuboff (1884–1969) was a notable patron of the arts and education. Zuboff's city mansion served as a meeting place for the capital's artistic bohemia. "Akhmatova prophesied to me": Anna Akhmatova's prophetic gift is an important part of the myth surrounding the name of one of Russia's greatest poets of the twentieth century.

10. Как вы когда-то разборчивы были / 10. How fastidious were you once (pp. 250–51)
This epigraph is taken from "Kurtku potërtuiu s belich'im mekhom . . ." ("A worn jacket with a squirrel fur lining," 1922), a poem by Ivanov's once friend, once foe Georgy Adamovich (see above). Ivanov's choice of an epigraph for his poem marked a period of reconciliation in their relationship, soon to be ended when Ivanov attacked Adamovich's Soviet sympathies, which Ivanov considered deplorable and irreconcilable with the position of an émigré poet and thinker. "Nuits": Nuits-Saint-Georges, a wine produced in the eponymous commune in the Côte de Nuits region of Burgundy, France.

1943–1958
POEMS

Published in September 1958, only several days after the author's death, *1943–1958. Poems* did not quite become Ivanov's "swan song" (to the extent that this cliché can be applied to Ivanov, that dubious distinction should certainly be given to his *Posthumous Diary*). It did, however, become the last collection of poems fully prepared and authorized by Ivanov in what was left of his lifetime.

1943–1958. Poems was put out in the United States by a publishing branch of *Novyi zhurnal* (*The New Review*). As has already been pointed out, in the post–WWII history of Russian émigré letters, the U.S.–based *Novyi zhurnal* (established in 1942 and still being produced) was—and to some degree still is—the living symbol of the continuity between the European phase of the Russian diaspora (after it had fallen victim to the ascent of Nazi Germany on the one hand and the USSR's expansion to the West on the other) and its newfound home in America. The book opens with a perceptive and compelling apology for Ivanov's ambivalent and complex "nihilism" from the pen of Roman Gul' (1896–1986), a longtime champion of his poetry and a personal friend. A distinguished émigré writer, literary critic, and memoirist, Gul' was to become *Novyi zhurnal's* editor-in-chief. Efforts by Gul' were not in vain, as some of Ivanov's contemporary critics leapt to dismiss his latest book using the same premise used by Gul' to extol it. It soon became clear, however, that a new—and to some observers unforeseen—generation of Ivanov's readers and critics had already arrived. The appearance of *1943–1958. Poems* in print was met with the appreciation of Vyacheslav Zavalishin and Vladimir Markov (see below), both representatives of the so-called "second" wave of Russian emigration to the West (an inevitably imperfect umbrella term describing post–WWII exiles from the Soviet Union). Seemingly belonging to an already turned page in the book of Russian culture both at home and abroad, Ivanov's poetry unexpectedly struck a chord with a group of readers whose emotional and cultural upbringing had no obvious connection with that of a poet who had frequently been dismissed as a living relic. This encounter "above the barriers" presaged Ivanov's posthumous return to and lasting popularity, first in the Perestroika-era Soviet Union, and then subsequently in today's Russia.

The present selection from *1943–1958. Poems* contains those of Ivanov's verses that were collected under that cover for the first time, not those republished.

Портрет без сходства (Игра судьбы. Игра добра и зла) / A Portrait Without Likeness (A game of fate. A game of good and evil) (pp. 254–56)
> First published in *Novyi zhurnal* in 1951.

RAYON DE RAYONNE (pp. 256–57)
> First published in *Novyi zhurnal* in 1955. "Mirrors reflect each other, / [m]utually distorting their reflections": Ivanov was singularly fond of echoing other poets and incorporating references to different literary texts into his poetry, and in the opening poem of his final verse collection he sardonically repeats one of the most famous lines of his own (see the poem opening with these lines in *A Portrait Without Likeness* [1950] and also "'Yellow violet'—sounds like 'viola'" in this collection). "And a rooster, awe-stricken / [g]ives ear to the harp of a Seraph": here Ivanov mockingly paraphrases a programmatic Pushkinian pronouncement on the vocation of a poet (see Pushkin's *"V chasy zabav il' prazdnoi skuki . . ."* ("During hours of merrymaking or idle boredom," 1830). Pushkin's lofty, neo-classical image—an awe-stricken poet paying heed to the voice of a Seraph—is lowered considerably in Ivanov's version, in which the poet is replaced by a lowly rooster (an allegory of a poet's position in the universe of Ivanov's own devising).

Вот более иль менее / Well, more or less (pp. 258–59)
> First published in *Novyi zhurnal* in 1955.

Что мне нравится — того я не имею / What I like—I don't possess (pp. 260–61)
> First published in *Novyi zhurnal* in 1953.

На полянке поутру / In a clearing in the morning dew (pp. 262–63)
> First published in *Novyi zhurnal* in 1954.

Художников развязная мазня / Artists' unbridled daubs (pp. 264–65)
> First published in *Novyi zhurnal* in 1954.

Дневник / Diary (pp. 266–67)
> First published in *Novyi zhurnal* in 1952. In both Russian and English the idiom "the salt of the earth," employed by Ivanov here, originates from the Sermon on the Mount (Matthew 5:13). In the context of the poem it designates the best representative of a nation repressed, killed, or exiled—or, as Ivanov puts it here, "[s]trewn about—swept away."

Калитка закрылась со скрипом / The gate closed with a creak (pp. 268–69)
> First published in *Novyi zhurnal* in 1954.

Эмалевый крестик в петлице / Small enamel cross in his lapel (pp. 270–71)
> First published in *Novyi zhurnal* in 1951. This is decidedly one of Ivanov's most recognizable poetic utterances, one of his signature pieces. Those portrayed here are, of course, the doomed Imperial family—the Romanovs—who were shot by the Bolsheviks in 1918. "Small enamel cross in his lapel": an automatic honoree of many a distinction and decoration, Nicholas II was particularly fond of wearing a cross of St. George, arguably the most prestigious distinction for soldiers and officers alike in the Russian Imperial Army.
>
> It should be stressed that Ivanov, author of the unfinished novel *Third Rome* (1929, 1931) and *Book of the Last Reign* (1933)—both of which mercilessly critique the doomed empire's highest circles—nourished no illusions about the last Russian emperor's abilities as a statesman (see also "Beclouded by lackluster glory" in this collection). The poem's ability to bring into sharp focus the intimate, human essence of what is, after all, a portrait of a family soon to be murdered after being assembled as if to pose for a group photograph, is nothing short of remarkable.

Теперь, когда я сгнил и черви обглодали / Now that I've decayed and worms have picked me (pp. 272–73)
> First published in *Novyi zhurnal* in 1951.

Смилостивилась погода / The weather had mercy (pp. 274–75)
> First published in *Novyi zhurnal* in 1957.

«Желтофиоль» — похоже на виолу / "Yellow violet"—sounds like "viola" (pp. 276–77)
> First published in *Novyi zhurnal* in 1954.

Этой жизни нелепость и нежность / Passing by the absurdity and tenderness (pp. 278–79)
> First published in *Novyi zhurnal* in 1951.

Мелодия становится цветком / Melody becomes a flower (pp. 280–81)
> First published in *Novyi zhurnal* in 1951. "Mist . . . Taman . . . The desert gives heed to God // [a]nd Lermontov alone comes out onto the road": the aural, if not semantic, imprint of the Russian word "mist" (compare *"tuman"* and *"Taman,"* the latter being a toponym) paves the way for Ivanov's invocation of one of the short stories making up Mikhail Lermontov's novel *Geroi nashego*

vremeni (*A Hero of Our Time*, 1839–41). It also alludes to his celebrated lyric, "*Vykhozhu odin ia na dorogu . . .*" ("I come out alone upon a highroad," 1841), considered by many readers to be his poetic farewell written in anticipation of his untimely (though eerily inevitable) death in a duel at the improbable age of twenty-seven. Lermontov's eventual appearance at the end of the poem is carefully prepared through an accumulation of details pertaining to his biography in the poem's second stanza.

Полутона рябины и малины / Half-tones of rowan and raspberry (pp. 282–83)

Vladimir Markov – scholar, historian of Russian modernism, critic, poet, and Los Angeles–based American academic of Russian extraction who made his way to the U.S. after being taken prisoner of war by the Nazis at an early stage in the siege of Leningrad. He first became one of Ivanov's most trusted correspondents and subsequently one of the most vocal and perceptive advocates of his poetry. The two men never met in person, but the Ivanov-Markov letters not only paint a vivid—if at times hardly flattering—picture of Ivanov's despondency (as well as his occasional ignorance and vitriol), but also contain a fascinating snapshot of an encounter of two strains of Russian culture, one belonging to pre-Revolutionary Russia and emigration (Ivanov), the other (Markov) representing a fresh current in Russian thought that had largely taken shape under the Soviet yoke and which was now peering with intense curiosity at a quintessential representative of a world forbidden by the Soviets.

The poem may be called a literary cryptogram, as it encodes a wide array of literary references that its dedicatee—as well as its reader—is invited to decipher. The poem's text is replete with echoes of other poets' work and references to their fates; scholars and commentators underline that such allusions occupy a principal place in Ivanov's poetics. Among those referenced in the poem are Goethe (or rather, Aleksey Konstantinovich Tolstoy's Russian version of Goethe's "The Bride of Corinth," 1797), Pushkin (Evlega is the name of a heroine of an Ossianic poem written in 1814; the "tremulous does" as well as the line "night mist descends on Georgia" paraphrase lines from Pushkin's *Poltava* (1828–29) and "*Na kholmakh Gruzii lezhit nochnaia mgla . . .*" ["On the hills of Georgia rests nocturnal gloom," 1829], respectively). Pyatigorsk, as well as other token details, reminds one of final phases of Lermontov's life, especially his untimely death in the vicinity of this town in northern Caucasus in 1841. The poem's closing distich is both an allusion to an old romance popular in Russia and also a reference to a rose, a signature image of Ivanov's poetry as well as that of the once madly popular self-proclaimed genius Igor' Severianin (Igor' Vasilievich Lotarev, 1887–1941). Mikhail Kuzmin is another noticeable presence in the poem (Ivanov once stated that Pushkin and Kuzmin had exerted a defining influence on him as a poet, and he never disavowed this confession). The rich allusive import of this poem has become subject of a small but significant body of scholarly works, with Vladimir Markov's and Andrei Arieff's contributions being most illuminating and significant. The poem's formal attributes allow it to be classified as a simplified sonnet with a coda.

Солнце село и краски погасли / The sun has set and the colors faded (pp. 284–85)
First published in *Novyi zhurnal* in 1951. "Beautiful Lady" is a key concept in the poetic universe of Aleksandr Blok's mysticism, prominently featured in his cycle *"Stikhi o Prekrasnoi Dame"* ("Verses About the Beautiful Lady," 1904). Blok, Russia's greatest Symbolist poet, derived his concept of eternal feminine from the idealist philosophy of Sofia compounded by the philosopher and poet Vladimir Solovyov (1853–1900). For Blok and his friend/rival Andrey Bely, Lyubov Mendeleeva-Blok (1881–1939), Blok's wife, became the embodiment of "Prekrasnaya Dama."

Стало тревожно-прохладно / In the garden it turned (pp. 286–87)
First published in *Novyi zhurnal* in 1956.

Так, занимаясь пустяками / And so, occupied with trifles (pp. 288–89)
First published in *Novyi zhurnal* in 1956.

Нет в России даже дорогих могил / In Russia there aren't even beloved graves (pp. 290–91)
Ivanov's friendship and voluminous correspondence with the dedicatee of this poem (Roman Gul', who was also the author of the introduction to this volume of Ivanov's verses; see above) began when Gul' was a secretary at *Novyi zhurnal*.

Ещё я нахожу очарованье / I still find enchantment (pp. 292–93)
First published in *Novyi zhurnal* in 1956.

Полу-жалость. Полу-отвращение / Half-compassion, half-revulsion (pp. 294–95)
First published in *Novyi zhurnal* in 1953.

Как обидно—чудным даром / How painful—to possess (pp. 296–97)
First published in *Novyi zhurnal* in 1951.

Иду—и думаю о разном / I stroll along, thinking of this and that (pp. 298–99)
First published in *Novyi zhurnal* in 1957.

Свободен путь под Фермопилами / The passage is free at Thermopylae (pp. 300–01)
First published in *Novyi zhurnal* in 1957. Ivanov's reference to the Battle of Thermopylae is in effect a sardonic reference to the Russian Empire's failed aspirations to become the center of the Orthodox Christianity, to "restore the cross over Hagia Sophia" (the Cathedral of Constantinople, one of the most revered shrines of Eastern Christianity dating from 1453, today a mosque in modern-day Istanbul), and to gain dominion over the Bosporus and the Dardanelles straits. The conservative thinkers Konstantin Nikolaevich Leontiev (1831–1891) and Fedor Ivanovich Tiutchev (1803–1873) were among the famous proponents of this quixotic quest (Tiutchev is also one of Russia's most illustrious metaphysical poets). "Slipping past the sober and the drunk, [s]he sits down by the window. // 'Breathing perfume and mist, [s]he sits down by the window'": this extended quotation is taken from "The Unknown Lady" ("Neznakomka," 1906), one of Blok's lyrical masterpieces. The poem's last two quatrains complete Ivanov's juxtaposition of old Russia's aspirations and its present state: blissfully unaware of the rich cultural substratum upon which their daily life is built, pretty members of the youth Communist organization (the "Komsomol girls" of the poem) have

unwittingly inherited the mythology that only an émigré and outsider of Ivanov's ilk can appreciate fully.

Я хотел бы улыбнуться / I would like to smile (pp. 302–03)
> First published in *Novyi zhurnal* in 1951.

Всё на свете не беда / All the world's not here nor there (pp. 304–05)
> First published in *Novyi zhurnal* in 1954.

Я научился понемногу / I've learned slowly, bit by bit (pp. 306–07)
> First published in *Novyi zhurnal* in 1951.

Уплывают маленькие ялики / Little skiffs float off (pp. 308–09)
> First published in *Novyi zhurnal* in 1956.

Сознанье, как море, не может молчать / Consciousness, like the sea, cannot remain silent (pp. 310–11)
> First published in *Novyi zhurnal* in 1954.

Стоят сады в сияньи белоснежном / The orchards stand in the snow-white glow (pp. 312–13)
> First published in *Novyi zhurnal* in 1953.

Всё туман. Бреду в тумане я / It's all a fog. I wander about in a fog (pp. 314–15)
> First published in *Novyi zhurnal* in 1953.

Четверть века прошло заграницей / A quarter-century passed abroad (pp. 316–17)
> First published in *Novyi zhurnal* in 1951. *"V Peterburge my soidemsia snova . . ."* ("In Petersburg we will come together again," 1920) is a poem by a friend of Ivanov's spirited literary youth Osip Emilievich Mandelstam (1891–1938). One of Russia's greatest twentieth-century poets, he was the victim of a prolonged and sadistic cat-and-mouse game carried out by Stalin and his henchmen. A recognized masterpiece of Mandelstam's mature lyricism, the poem is a piercing promise of an inevitable return to the city where the poet and his friends spent their youth. Ivanov's certitude concerning the assured fullfillment of "the prophesy of a dead friend," therefore, must be envisaged on a metaphysical plane, or putting it simply, as a long-delayed, beyond-the-grave reunification.

Эти сумерки вечерние / I recalled those twilight evenings (pp. 318–19)
> First published in *Novyi zhurnal* in 1954. "Kostroma province": Kostroma is a picturesque city on the upper bank of the Volga, approximately 200 miles to the northeast of Moscow. For all its comeliness, in this poem Kostroma province represents a Russian backwater. "The Black Hundreds": an umbrella term for all of Russia's right-wing, ultraconservative, chauvinistic, monarchist, and anti-Semitic organizations, the most influential of them being the Union of the Russian People. These groups attempted to play a part in politics from 1905 to 1917.

Овеянный тускнеющею славой / Beclouded by lackluster glory (pp. 320–21)
> First published in *Novyi zhurnal* in 1955. It might be difficult to appreciate the fact that the two-headed eagle—Russia's heraldic symbol since 1472—was little more than an obsolete relic of a ruined empire at the time Ivanov wrote this poem.

Голубая речка / Sky-blue rivulet (pp. 322–23)
> First published in *Novyi zhurnal* in 1955.

Луны начищенный пятак / The moon's shining five-kopeck coin (pp. 324–25)
> First published in *Novyi zhurnal* in 1954.

Звёзды меркли в бледнеющем небе / The stars faded in the paling sky (pp. 326–27)
> First published in *Novyi zhurnal* in 1953.

Белая лошадь бредёт без упряжки / A white horse roams without a harness (pp. 328–29)
> First published in 1954.

Нечего тебе тревожиться / There is no reason for you to worry (pp. 330–31)
> First published in *Novyi zhurnal* in 1957. "Uspensky" and "Volkov" are both cemeteries in St. Petersburg, and together with references to the sands of Golodai Island, St. Isaac's Cathedral, and the frozen Neva river, these names work to create a condensed vision of a hypothetical reunification with Russia, if only in death. Many denizens of revolutionary Petersburg knew that Golodai Island—along with unknown holes in the ice of the Neva—became a final resting place for the victims of Bolshevik mass killings committed at the height of the so-called Red Terror.

Цветущих яблонь тень сквозная / The transparent shade of apple blossoms (pp. 332–33)
> First published in *Novyi zhurnal* in 1953.

Тускнеющий вечерный час / The dimming evening hour (pp. 334–35)
> First published in *Novyi zhurnal* in 1953.

На границе снега и таянья / On the border of snow and melt (pp. 336–37)
> First published in *Novyi zhurnal* in 1951.

Закат в полнеба занесён / The sunset ranges half the sky (pp. 338–39)
> First published in *Novyi zhurnal* in 1956. "Lenore" (or "Leonore," 1773) is the name of an eponymous ballad by Gottfried August Bürger (German, 1747–1794) featuring a maiden taken away by her ghostly groom. Bürger's "Lenore" became a quintessential text of European Romanticism; it was much translated, paraphrased, and referenced in Russia.

Я твёрдо решился и тут же забыл / I firmly decided and right then forgot (pp. 340–41)
> First published in *Novyi zhurnal* in 1953.

Насладись, пока не поздно / Take pleasure, before it is too late (pp. 342–43)
> First published in *Novyi zhurnal* in 1953.

Поэзия: искусственная поза / Poetry: an artificial pose (pp. 344–45)
> First published in *Novyi zhurnal* in 1952. "The Upas Tree" is a mythical tree of death, as well as the title and the subject of an eponymous poem by Pushkin (1828).

Мне весна ничего не сказала / Spring said nothing to me (pp. 346–47)
> First published in *Novyi zhurnal* in 1958.

Почти не видно человека среди сиянья и шелков / A man is almost lost midst radiance and silks (pp. 348–49)
> First published in *Novyi zhurnal* in 1951. Ivanov's favorite artist, Watteau, was born in Valenciennes in northern France. "As a Russian Demon in the Caucasus":

here Watteau is linked to Lermontov by way of Russia's great Modernist painter Mikhail Aleksandrovich Vrubel (1856–1910), who illustrated Lermontov's narrative poem *Demon* (1829–1840). Ivanov's chain of associations, therefore, becomes clear: thinking of the Caucasus as the place of Lermontov's reluctant but fecund exile, Ivanov attempts to liken the France of his own exile to that of Watteau.

Ветер с Невы. Леденеющий март / Wind from the Neva. Freezing March (pp. 350–51)

First published in 1953. Chukhloma is a distant provincial town in Kostroma.

Просил. Но никто не помог / He pleaded, but no one helped (pp. 352–53)

First published in 1952.

Бредёт старик на рыбный рынок / An old man plods to the fish market (pp. 354–55)

First published in *Novyi zhurnal* in 1957. "The spitting image of Wrangel": Baron Nikolai Nikolaevich Wrangel (1880–1915, brother of the last Commander in Chief of the White Army) was an art historian who collaborated with the Acmeist journal *Apollo* (1909–1917). Later in his life Ivanov claimed Wrangel as a mentor.

Жизнь пришла в порядок / Life has come together (pp. 356–57)

First published in *Novyi zhurnal* in 1954.

Меняется прическа и костюм / Dress and hairstyles change (pp. 358–59)

First published in *Novyi zhurnal* in 1952.

Волны шумели: «Скорее, скорее!» / The waves called: "Faster, faster"! (pp. 360–61)

First published in *Novyi zhurnal* in 1954. "Lorelei": "Die Lore Lay" (1801) is a ballad by Clemens Brentano (German, 1778–1842) which interprets the legend of a water nymph associated with a rock on the eastern bank of the river Rhine in Germany. According to the tradition, this river siren was wont to lure wanderers to their deaths.

Я люблю безнадежный покой / I love hopeless peace (pp. 362–63)

First published in *Novyi zhurnal* in 1954. *Songs without Words* (*Romances sans paroles*, 1874) is a book of poetry by Paul Verlaine. Innokentiy Fyodorovich Annensky (1856–1909) was a poet, playwright, critic, and translator who belonged to the "older" generation of Russian Symbolists. Nikolai Gumilyov (see above), one of the two leaders of the Acmeist movement in Russian poetry, was Annensky's disciple and Ivanov's mentor.

О, нет, не обращаюсь к миру я / No, I don't speak to the world (pp. 364–65)

First published in *Novyi zhurnal* in 1951.

Если бы я мог забыться / If only I could sink into oblivion (pp. 366–67)

First published in *Novyi zhurnal* in 1951. The motif of longed-for oblivion once again develops the main theme of Lermontov's "*Vykhozhu odin ia na dorogu . . .* ," one of Ivanov's favorite points of reference.

Мне больше не страшно. Мне томно / I'm not afraid any more. I'm listless (pp. 368–69)

First published in *Novyi zhurnal* in 1952.

То, что было, и то, чего не было / What has been, and what never was (pp. 370–71)

First published in *Novyi zhurnal* in 1951.

Чем дольше живу я, тем менее / The longer I live the less (pp. 372–73)
> First published in *Novyi zhurnal* in 1953.

Всё на свете дело случая / In this world everything is a matter of chance (pp. 374–75)
> First published in *Novyi zhurnal* in 1956.

Здесь в лесах даже розы цветут / Here in the forests even roses bloom (pp. 376–77)
> First published in *Novyi zhurnal* in 1953.

Не станет ни Европы, ни Америки / Gone will be Europe and America (pp. 378–79)
> First published in *Novyi zhurnal* in 1953.

Всё на свете пропадает даром / All in this world is lost uselessly (pp. 380–81)
> First published in *Novyi zhurnal* in 1954.

Листья падали, падали, падали / The leaves fell, and fell, and fell (pp. 382–83)
> First published in *Novyi zhurnal* in 1955.

Ну, мало ли что бывает / Well, anything can happen (pp. 384–85)
> First published in *Novyi zhurnal* in 1954.

Всё представляю в блаженном тумане я / I conjure it all in a blessed mist
(pp. 386–87)
> First published in *Novyi zhurnal* in 1953. *Poor Folk* (1846), the debut work of
> Fyodor Dostoevsky (1821–1881), is an epistolary novel depicting the life of the
> poor and downtrodden Makar Devushkin and his neighbor Varvara. This work
> was heralded as a great event in the history of Russian literature by the poet, edi-
> tor, and critic Nikolay Nekrasov (1821–1877), as well as by the dominant liberal
> literary critic of the age, Vassarion Belinsky (1811–1848). Ivanov is correct to
> doubt his authorship of this witty, if grim, take on the title of Dostoevsky's novel:
> it belongs to the émigré critic, journalist, writer, and thinker Grigorii Adol'fovich
> Landau (1877–1941).

Не обманывают только сны / Only dreams do not deceive (pp. 388–89)
> First published in 1952.

На юге Франции прекрасны / In the south of France so fine (pp. 390–91)
> First published in *Novyi zhurnal* in 1956.

А ещё недавно было всё, что надо / Not so long ago we had everything (pp. 392–93)
> First published in 1953. Tatiana Grigorievna Terentieva (1906–1986) was the edi-
> tor of the New York–based Chekhov Publishing House, a major émigré publishing
> venture after World War II. Ivan Sergeevich Turgenev (1818–1883), one of Russia's
> preeminent novelists, created some of the most evocative and memorable works
> depicting the life of the Russian gentry before the abolition of serfdom in Russia. It
> should not be forgotten that Turgenev spent a great deal of his life in France.

Когда-нибудь, когда устанешь ты / Sometime, when you grow weary (pp. 394–95)
> First published in 1952.

Мы не молоды. Но и не стары / We are not young, yet neither are we old (pp. 396–97)
> First published in *Novyi zhurnal* in 1951.

Как всё бесцветно, всё безвкусно / How all is colorless, and tasteless (pp. 398–99)
> First published in *Novyi zhurnal* in 1951. The "Demoniac" Lermontov-Vrubel
> connection has already been stressed by Ivanov in this collection (see above).

1. Ты не расслышала, а я не повторил / 1. You didn't make it out, I did not repeat (pp. 400–01)

> First published in *Novyi zhurnal* in 1955. The epigraph is borrowed from Ivanov's own poem "*Ne o liubvi proshu, ne o vesne poiu . . .*" ("It's not for love that I ask, it's not of spring that I sing," first published in 1921).

2. Распылённый мильоном мельчайших частиц / 2. Ground to a million miniscule particles (pp. 402–03)

> First published in *Novyi zhurnal* in 1954. Summer Garden is another actual detail of an idealized St. Petersburg cityscape envisaged in the opening poem of this cycle.

3. Вся сиянье, вся непостоянство / 3. All radiance, all inconstancy (pp. 404–05)

> First published in 1952.

4. Отзовись, кукушечка, яблочко, змеёныш / 4. Say something, my cuckoo, little apple, baby snake (pp. 406–07)

> First published in *Novyi zhurnal* in 1956. The epigraph is taken from "Toska pripominania" ("Sadness of Recollection," 1910) by Annensky (see above).

5. Может быть, умру я в Ницце / 5. Perhaps I shall die in Nice (pp. 408–09)

> First published in *Novyi zhurnal* in 1954.

Зима идёт своим порядком / Winter goes along its usual way (pp. 410–11)

> First published in 1957.

Скучно, скучно мне до одуренья / I'm bored, bored silly (pp. 412–13)

> First published in *Novyi zhurnal* in 1957.

Накипевшая за годы / Building up for years (pp. 414–15)

> First published in *Novyi zhurnal* in 1957. The Mr. A and Mr. B of the poem come courtesy of a children's nursery rhyme that does not have an exact parallel in English.

Туман. Передо мной дорога / Mist. The road in front of me (pp. 416–17)

> First published in *Novyi zhurnal* in 1957. Yet another poem containing—opening with it, in this particular case—a paraphrase of Lermontov's "*Vykhozhu odin ia na dorogu . . .*"

Отвлечённой сложностью персидского ковра / As the abstract complexity of a Persian rug (pp. 420–21)

> First published in *Novyi zhurnal* in 1957.

POSTHUMOUS DIARY

The selection comprising Ivanov's truly last collection of poetry was published by Irina Odoevtseva, his muse, wife, and subsequently widow, executrix, and editor. Contemporary editors of Ivanov's poetry point out that in a number of cases there simply are not any surviving manuscripts of the poems included in this collection, as Odoevtseva wrote them down from memory after her husband's death. *Posthumous Diary*, which chronicles Ivanov's gradual death, was first reproduced as a unified cycle in 1975.

Александр Сергеич, я о вас скучаю / Aleksandr Sergeich, how much I miss you (pp. 424–25)

> First published in *Novyi zhurnal* in 1958. The strikingly informal (yet at the same time respectful enough) manner in which Ivanov chooses to address Russia's greatest poet is characteristic of this entire cycle of poems. While not omitting the poet's first name, Ivanov slightly shortens his patronymic (compare "Sergeyevich," which is the full form [stressed on the second syllable], with the decidedly less formal "Sergeich"). The import of Ivanov's action is clear: the "hard dying" that Ivanov shares with Pushkin brings the younger poet closer to his predecessor and renders excessive formality superficial. Another detail should not escape the attention of a committed reader: if Mikhail Lermontov, that brooding *enfant terrible* of Russian poetry, can be said to have been the tutelary deity of Ivanov's penultimate collection of poems, it is Pushkin whom Ivanov chooses to evoke on his deathbed. Pushkin died a slow and painful death after being shot through the liver in a duel he fought to defend his and his wife's honor.

Кошка крадётся по светлой дорожке / A cat slinks along a bright pathway (pp. 426–27)

> First published in *Novyi zhurnal* in 1958.

Я жил как будто бы в тумане / I lived as if it were in a fog (pp. 428–29)

> First published in *Novyi zhurnal* in 1958.

Мне уж не придётся впредь / From now on, I won't have the need (pp. 430–31)

> First published in Novyi zhurnal in 1958. "Before one is to die, / [o]ne's got to talk a bit": Ivanov is echoing *"Pered tem, kak umeret'* . . ." ("Before one is to die," 1930), his own poem from *Roses* (1931). The admission ". . . 'tis time, my friend, 'tis time!" is borrowed from Pushkin's poem ". . . 'tis time, my friend, 'tis time! My heart begs peace" (1834).

В громе ваших барабанов / I kept my distance (pp. 432–33)

> First published in *Novyi zhurnal* in 1958, like all five poems reproduced above it is dated, "August 1958."

А может быть, ещё и не конец / But maybe it's not quite the end (pp. 434–35)

> First published in *Novyi zhurnal* in 1958. Hyères, a commune in the Var department (southeastern France), did become Ivanov's resting place. "The Neva and Volga, the Nevsky and the Arbat": just as the rivers Neva and Volga define St. Petersburg and Central Russia, the lively avenues Nevsky and Arbat define St.

Petersburg and Moscow, respectively.

Воскресенье. Удушья прилив и отлив / Sunday. The ebb and flow of suffocation (pp. 436–37)

First published in *Novyi zhurnal* in 1958.

Ку-ку-реку или бре-ке-ке-ке / Cock-a-doodle-do or ribb-be-et (pp. 438–39)

First published in *Novyi zhurnal* in 1958.

Аспазия, всегда Аспазия / Aspasia, always Aspasia (pp. 440–41)

First published in *Novyi zhurnal* in 1958. Aspasia (470 BC–400 BC) was the mistress (or possibly wife) of Pericles of Athens. She was the mother of Pericles the Younger, an Athenian general. Nausicaa is a character in Homer's *Odyssey*: the beautiful daughter of King Alcinous and Queen Arete, she appears in Book Six to lead Odysseus to her parents, who provide ships to Odysseus for the final leg of his journey home to Ithaca.

Ночь, как Сахара, как ад, горяча / The night is hot, like the Sahara, like hell (pp. 442–43)

First published in *Novyi zhurnal* in 1958.

Ночных часов тяжёлый рой / The heavy swarm of night hours (pp. 444–45)

First published in *Novyi zhurnal* in 1959, dated "August 1958." "[I]t is my soul crying": coupled with the vision of a violent death invoked at the poem's end, the image of a crying or weeping soul puts one in mind of Homer, and specifically, of *The Iliad*—its numerous depictions of deaths on the battlefield before Troy are frequently followed by portrayals of souls weeping as they are forced to part with their bodies and descend into Hades.

На барабане б мне погреметь / I would like to beat out on drums (pp. 446–47)

First published in *Novyi zhurnal* in 1959.

Дымные пятна соседних окон / Smoky blotches of neighbor windows (pp. 448–49)

First published in *Novyi zhurnal* in 1959.

Меня уносит океан / The ocean carries me off (pp. 450–51)

First published in *Novyi zhurnal* in 1959.

Зачем, как шальные, свистят соловьи / Why do the nightingales whistle wildly (pp. 452–53)

First published in *Novyi zhurnal* in 1959.

Все розы увяли. И пальма замёрзла / All the roses faded. And the palm tree froze (pp. 454–55)

First published in *Novyi zhurnal* in 1959.

В зеркале сутулый, тощий / In the mirror—bent, emaciated (pp. 456–57)

First published in *Novyi zhurnal* in 1959.

Побрили Кикапу в последний раз / They shaved the Kickapoo for the last time (pp. 458–59)

First published in *Novyi zhurnal* in 1959. The poem opens with an approximate quotation from a poem entitled *"Konets Kickapoo"* ("The End of Kickapoo," 1915) by Tikhon Vasilievich Churilin (1885–1946).

Было всё — и тюрьма и сума / There has been everything—prison and tramping (pp. 460–61)

> First published in *Novyi zhurnal* in 1959.

Пароходы в море тонут / Ships drown in the sea (pp. 462–63)

> First published in *Novyi zhurnal* in 1959.

В ветвях олеандровых трель соловья / The nightingale's trill in the oleander branches (pp. 464–65)

> First published in *Novyi zhurnal* in 1959.

Строка за строкой. Тоска. Облака / Line after line. Longing. Clouds (pp. 466–67)

> First published in *Novyi zhurnal* in 1960. Ivanov borrows the epigraph from his own poem "*Svoboden put' pod Fermopilami . . .*" ("The passage is free at Thermopylae," *1943–1958. Poems*), and later the present poem becomes a distorted mirror reflection of that earlier piece. Like Pushkin and like Ivanov, the French novelist Marcel Proust (1871–1922) died a long, painful death. Proust was one of the great novelists of the twentieth century, and his work influenced such master writers as James Joyce and Vladimir Nabokov. Although he wrote much fiction and literary criticism, Proust is remembered for his unfinished monumental novel *À la recherche du temps perdu* (*Remembrance of Things Past*), some seven volumes and 3,000 pages long. The work's focus is the attempt to recapture and immortalize all-destroying time through memory and art.

Из спальни уносят лампу / The lamp is taken from the bedroom (pp. 468–69)

> First published in 1927.

А что такое вдохновенье / And just what is inspiration (pp. 470–71)

> First published in *Novyi zhurnal* in 1960. Azrael is the Archangel of Death in the Islamic tradition. "*Tsitseron*" ("Cicero," 1830) is a poem by Fedor Tiutchev, which states that he who has been on this earth during a time of trouble will be invited to join the righteous ones at their heavenly feast.

Вас осуждать бы стал с какой же стати я / Why should I stand in judgment over you (pp. 472–73)

> First published in *Novyi zhurnal* in 1960.

За столько лет такого маянья / After so many years of such toiling (pp. 474–75)

> First published in 1960.

До нелепости смешно / It is ridiculous to absurdity (pp. 476–77)

> First published in 1960. "Purgatory": since the Orthodox Christian tradition rejects the notion of Purgatory, our English equivalent of Ivanov's invocation of sinners' beyond-the-grave torments as seen by those who still have a chance to be saved (compare "*khozhdenie po mukam*") can only be an approximate one. Mikhail Kuzmin popularized this topic in his masterful imitations of folk narratives depicting visions and visitations ("Holy Mother of God Visits Hell," etc.).

Отчаянье я превратил в игру / I've turned despair into a game (pp. 478–79)

> First published in 1958.

Для голодных собак понедельник / For hungry dogs it's Monday (pp. 480–81)

> First published in 1958.

Теперь бы чуточку беспечности / Now I'd like a bit of being carefree (pp. 482–83)
    First published in 1959. Pavlovsk: see above.
Вечер. Может быть, последний / Evening. Perhaps my last (pp. 484–85)
    First published in 1959.
Вот ёлочка. А вот и белочка / Here's a little spruce. And here a little squirrel
(pp. 486–87)
    First published in 1975.
Если б время остановить / If time could be stopped (pp. 488–89)
    First published in 1972.
Ликование вечной, блаженной весны / The exultation of eternal, blessed spring
(pp. 490–91)
    First published in 1975. The image of his mentor and friend Nikolai Gumilyov
    (see above) evidently stayed with Ivanov until his last days. Lethe, one of five
    rivers that run through Hades, is the river of oblivion and forgetfulness in Greek
    mythology.
Бороться против неизбежности / To me is not given to struggle (pp. 492–93)
    First published in 1975. "[Y]our black bow": a bow was a requisite part of
    Odoevtseva's appearance in the days of her youth in Petersburg-Petrograd when
    she first met Ivanov (Odoevtseva mentions this bow in her poetic self-portrait).
В небе нежно тают облака / Clouds tenderly melt in the sky (pp. 494–95)
    First published in 1975.
Во сне я думаю о разном / In my sleep I think of various things (pp. 496–97)
    First published in 1975.
Поговори со мной ещё немного / Speak to me yet a little more (pp. 498–99)
    First published in 1975. "Your lilting, light voice": Ivanov's last poem is addressed
    to Odoevtseva, whose voice and minor speech defect, which Ivanov found
    endearing, are evoked here.

УКАЗАТЕЛЬ ЗАГЛАВИЙ И ПЕРВЫХ СТРОК

INDEX OF TITLES AND FIRST LINES